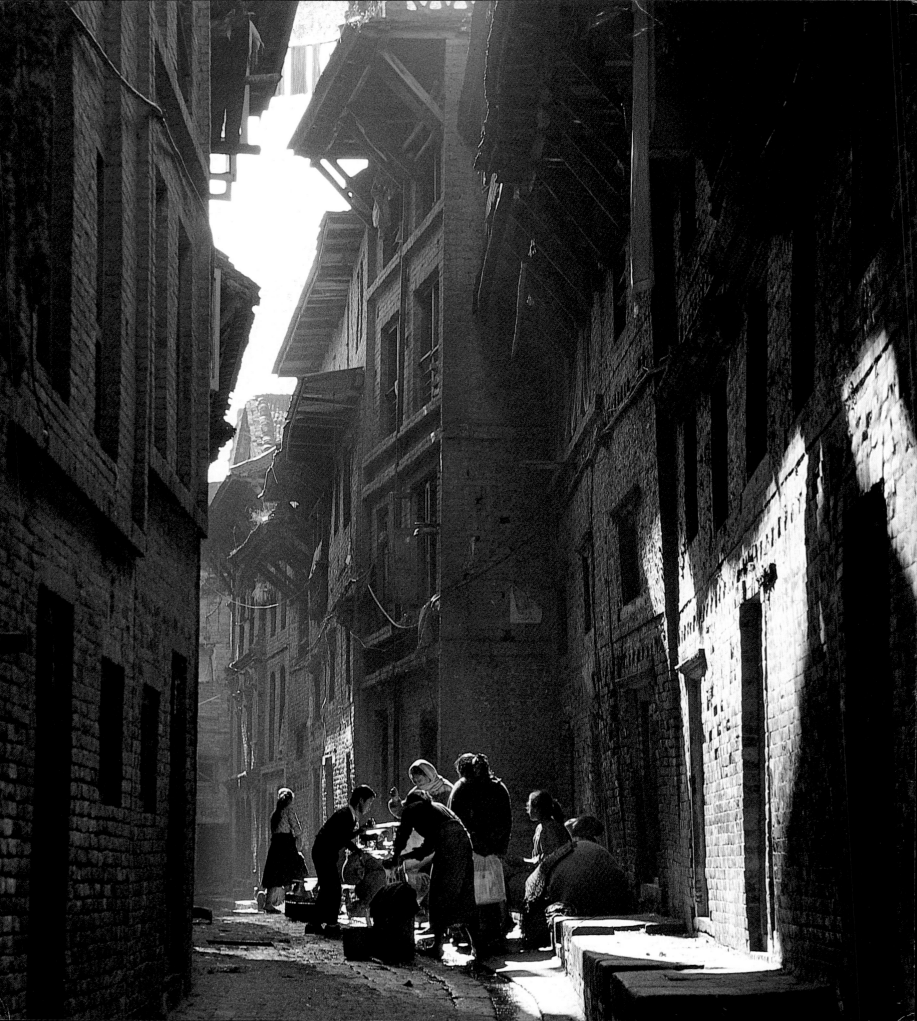

STAFFORD CLIFF

THE WAY WE LIVE

An Ultimate Treasury for Global Design Inspiration

PHOTOGRAPHS BY
GILLES DE CHABANEIX

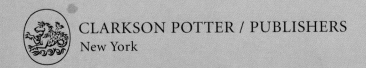

CLARKSON POTTER / PUBLISHERS
New York

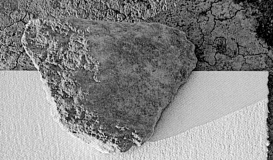

INTRODUCTION

Homes and lifestyles

LOCATION

BUILDING

DESIGN

DECORATION

DETAIL

LIVING

ON THE VERY FIRST PAGE OF THIS BOOK there is an oddly mysterious picture of a man, apparently standing before half-open windows. The surreal quality of the image is due to its being, in fact, a *trompe-l'œil* feature on a façade in Rome. Yet, there is much in the image that fascinates us. Why is he there? What is he looking at? And can we see it, too? In a larger sense, this is a visual metaphor of the contents of this book, an account of how artifice is employed to make our environment a pleasanter place to live in – we design; we build; we decorate and embellish; and, hopefully, we have the freedom to take delight in what we have created. The windows behind the figure of the man are half-open, hinting at the interior on the other side; and, effectively, much of the subject-matter of the chapters which follow is perceived from the position of a person on the outside looking in. But the man is also looking out to a wider perspective, just as this remarkable photographic archive draws its material from homes and lifestyles around the world.

This is a book about living in the broadest and narrowest of senses; thus, it ranges from the bigger picture of humanity placing its imprint on the planet to the illustration of intimate details of decoration and design, to the day-to-day enjoyment and celebration of our homes and their surroundings. In their evocation of so many different and varied styles of living, these photographs constitute a unique body of detailed design inspiration, a record of how we live that is also a guide to where we might live in our various environments: by water, on the land, in villages, towns and cities around the world.

For the first time, we can observe here the solutions that individuals, families and whole communities have found to major concerns: choice of location; siting and building; decoration of interiors; cultivation of the areas around the home. Given the enormous range of places and dwellings illustrated on the pages of this book, it is striking and perhaps reassuring to see patterns emerging in the way people do things in very different habitats. At every stage in the broad processes of building, embellishing, refining and enjoying the final result, the

MOROCCO   SCOTLAND

connections and parallels between myriad national, regional and historical styles are almost more evident than the predictable

differences. The same attention to detail can clearly inform the arrangement of a dining-room in a modest Mexican home as it does in an exclusive club in Buenos Aires. Here, humble settings and structures, artefacts and designs commingle with the grandiose, elaborate and exclusive, sometimes revealing surprising similarities: an impoverished New York tenement interior, restored for historical purposes, finds echoes in fashionable London and Paris kitchens whose owners have a taste for the utensils of the pre-plastic age; a narrow street in Katmandu, essence of urban intensity, has its counterparts in Rome and Stockholm. Yet all these places are treated with the same sympathetic eye; the shack

BALI   MEXICO

or cottage interior, cheaply furnished, may yield as much decorative inspiration as the grandest of *palazzi* or the most exclusive of metropolitan apartments.

If there is a bias in this book, perhaps it is towards environments coated with the patinas of time and occupation, places and settings that have evolved and tell a story rather than those that have just emerged fresh from the interior designer's computer. This is really a book about what people make of their environment in their own way, with their own possessions, many or few, in their instinctive use of colours and materials, in the way they inhabit the spaces they have made their own. Old and new, man-made and man-found co-exist happily; the textures, patinas and accretions of use and age are the visible expressions of our will to live as we wish.

Inevitably, much of the imagery in the chapters which follow (apart from the final chapter) is of the inanimate – buildings, architectural detail, interior spaces and individual objects. Even so, there is something in the way the camera has been directed that emphasizes the human scale in everything photographed. Arrangements of objects, the disposition of furniture in a room, the detailing on a façade, all look peculiarly enticing, lived-in, and full of promise and inspiration. We are led down narrow streets – some orderly, others chaotic – through doorways, alleys, passages and entrances, always looking out for the prospect of something

NEPAL   PHILIPPINES

delightful beyond. That 'beyond' may be a sunlit square vibrant with neighbourhood life, a seafront lined with fishing vessels, a market full of fresh produce, or a gorgeously and extravagantly appointed room, magnificently framed through an arch or open door. Staircases and other transitional spaces, like passages or landings, are given due importance as they connect different spaces within the same home,

leading us on from room to room, placing the particular in the context of the general.

Through the sequence of chapters and their sub-sections, we encounter the whole gamut of lifestyle options; the first concerns are with location: natural sites, buildings both in groups and individual, markets, shops, bars, cafés and churches. The textures of outward appearance are illustrated in profusion: surfaces, patterns, arrangements, signs, decoration, presentation, and national, regional and historical styles. Inside the home, there are examples of rooms where we meet, where we relax and where we work, and all the details within them: doors, windows, lighting, colour, texture, displays of objects and works of art. Finally, there are the themes of living, of celebration, of making the most of what we have, grand or humble, of being part in some measure of the whole human achievement. A village in the Philippines celebrates its harvest festival with streets full of glowing arrangements of local produce; a Moroccan house coolly mixes the modern and

CHILOË   MEXICO

traditional in elegant interiors; an arrangement of shells looks dramatically decorative on a table top in Mauritius; two children in the dress of their region smile at the camera in a Mexican town; flowers are strewn across the bare floorboards for a Christmas feast in Sweden; and women in a Romanian village move their cooking utensils outdoors to prepare for a community wedding.

The plan of the book follows a simple progression: how we build in the community in different habitats; how we add to and refine to create our own lifestyle; and how we then inhabit what we have with the possessions we have gathered around us. As such, this is a sourcebook of thousands of possibilities: as we bring our finds home from flea-markets and yard sales, so what we see in other contexts, other cultures, can also affect our own lives. Choosing where we live is a starting-point: a beach house in Chile or on the west coast of France, or a loft space in Paris or New York? In what kind of terrain do we feel most at ease and in what kind of building? We may find the answer to our own questions in very different places: on a waterfront, by a lake, by a river, on an island, in hill villages, or in the midst of plantations or farmland. There are the urban alternatives: New York 'brownstones' and their near-cousins, English townhouses; converted industrial spaces

BALI   SUMBAWA

and high-rise apartment blocks; courtyard compounds in south-east Asia; and complexes of houses around the Mediterranean and in Africa

where each habitation seems organically connected to its neighbour.

From the larger issues of location and the making of the human imprint, we move to the more personal ones of self-projection within the home: interiors, decoration, arrangement and presentation. Here, within this Aladdin's Cave of choices and inspirations, are the contrasts of stark simplicity and sumptuous embellishment, minimal modernism and Baroque splendour, the self-consciously urbane and the authentically rustic, the classical and romantic, the rough and the smooth, the uniform and the eclectic. There are national, regional and historical styles: English Georgian and French Neoclassicism;

SALZBURG   GOA

Oriental minimalism and high ornament; colonial crossovers, where western tastes have mingled with the indigenous traditions; very personal looks and formal arrangements. All the schemes and arrangements illustrated are unique and many are very individual, yet how striking the underlying similarities in, say, the treatment of doors, staircases, windows, the arrangement of furniture, the choice of colour and material. Scandinavian and Oriental approaches commingle to produce a modernist interior in London; colonial furniture sits happily in a drawing-room in Versailles; a discreetly decorated bed-sitting-room in Morocco could easily inspire a home-maker in northern Europe.

And within whole interiors are revealed the details. In the fourth chapter are the minutiae of design and decoration: arrangements of objects on walls, in cupboards and on shelves; the placing of pictures or free-standing ornaments; the treatment of those awkward transitional spaces in the home, like staircases, corridors, entrance-halls and landings. Often there is some quirkiness in what we see, a lack of contrivance. Perhaps the colours are slightly faded, the materials showing wear and tear, the alignment not quite straight, condition not quite perfect. Wall displays, the disposition of ornaments, the little vignettes of personal memorabilia, all indicate 'living' rather than 'contrivance'. Usually, too, there is an implied meaning in what the camera has picked out – a personal history, a

QUEBEC   NICE

family tradition, an artist's concern for materials and textures, a respect for the vernacular.

Finally, the doorway from the home leads again to the outside; it is now the chance for interior life to mingle with the larger community. We leave the house for the loggia, the veranda, the patio, the courtyard, and the garden. Sometimes these moments of transition can be defined by nothing more than a table and

chairs set up almost at random in some agreeable spot; in other circumstances, custom and practice have dictated the making of something more like a fully furnished outside room.

Beyond the garden gate or front door lies the street, artery of communication and exchange, deserted at times, animated at others in small and large communities alike. Places of colour and creativity, real, living streets, squares and markets repay in abundance close attention to their details: shop fronts in their original state; mountains of produce; household goods, all displayed and presented with instinctive care. There is a joy in many of these places, a kind of celebration of the way humanity manages to remain positive about its future, in spite of vicissitudes and catastrophes. Fitting, then, that the book should close with the final ingredient, people going about their business, some self-conscious, some indifferent, but all making their contribution to the human achievement – the making of homes in a thousand different ways. We end our journey with a glorious burst of colour by the villagers of an island in the Philippines, ingeniously transforming their

IRELAND   ROME

homes in celebration of their harvest festival!

THE WAY WE LIVE | *CHAPTER TWO*

WHERE WE LIVE

Dwellings around the world

BY THE WATER
ON THE LAND
IN TOWN AND CITY
WINDOWS ON THE WORLD

THE DEVELOPMENT OF THE URGE TO BUILD shelter for ourselves and to create the necessary tools for construction must rank among the most important of mankind's great leaps forward: the transition from dwelling in caves or holes in the ground to assembling the wherewithal to create an entirely new edifice, to put, literally, roofs over our heads, is a cultural shift of seismic proportions. But however basic the human instinct to create habitations for the individual, the group or the community at large, the forms and styles of the final result are largely dictated by local conditions, the availability of wood, stone, clay, metal, and by the subsequent craftsmanship that brings the materials together.

Coastal hamlet to city centre: these two extremes represent only a fraction of the varied locations in which we can choose to live and create our individual lifestyles. Where we spend the major part of our lives is, of course, rarely entirely a matter of free choice; necessity, accident, and occasionally catastrophe can all play a part. But, in the locations illustrated on the pages which follow, much will engage our dreams and fantasies as we look upon man's remarkable ingenuity in finding solutions to living in very different environments.

Whether taking over a house previously occupied, with the patinas and characteristics of long occupation still somehow present, or building to our own tastes and imagination, there is a peculiar satisfaction in occupying an enclosed space in which our own order prevails against the unpredictability of the outside world. Some of these houses really do give the impression of having been set down on their sites almost in defiance of surrounding nature. Others lie easily in the folds of the landscape, their contours and materials configuring those of the earth from which they seem to spring. And whole towns and villages may look thus, as though they had burgeoned and grown together as living organisms, which indeed they have.

In contrast, some large conurbations can seem almost entirely divorced from the terrain on which they have been founded and over which they have gradually spread. The land beneath is seemingly compressed out of existence by the enormous layers of masonry and steel, marvellously evoked in Gilles de Chabaneix's photographs of large cities.

Yet within those towering walls lie imaginative and exciting living spaces: townhouses, apartments, lofts, penthouses, just as satisfying to their owners as the most stately plantation house to a rural landowner. Nor are all high concentrations of human habitation cut off from their immediate natural surroundings: the towers and battlements of the Berber dwellings of the Dra valley in Morocco reflect the colours and textures of the earth itself. Whatever the location, though, those illustrated in this chapter are all interesting and many are very beautiful.

Those of us who choose to live by water may reflect on the suitability of lake, river or the sea for the development of our lifestyles. Many of the waterside homes that form the subject of the first part of this chapter are clearly conceived as havens of peace by their owners. Isolated cottages, villas with verandas and terraces looking out to sea, or even apartments in sea-front towns represent a tempting alternative to city life. Then there is the special quality of the light and air that comes off the water, luminous and refreshing, a direct tonic after the grime and noise of a large city. Even the interiors in waterside locations can seem more intensely illuminated than their inland counterparts.

The types of dwelling in waterside locations are so varied as to represent a lifetime of choices in themselves. Even within the relatively constricted space devoted to this kind of living in these pages, there is sufficient variety to correspond to most of the moods and temperaments at play when we try to answer that all-important question: where shall I or we live? On the west coast of Ireland, amid the fells and lakes of Connemara, someone has clearly found the ideal home, if isolation is a primary need. The sense of being apart from the bustling crowds of town and city is

ÎLE DE RÉ

hugely increased by a location in a natural habitat of beauty and power, dominated by the watery stretches of the lake.

Other options, mentioned above and illustrated on the

following pages, extend the ideal of living by water to locations around the world, all of them attractive, yet very different. There is, for instance, a very special quality to life on an island – a concept in itself that immediately evokes strong feelings of apartness, yet also of being in touch with the larger forces of nature, of which the background sound of the sea provides a constant reminder.

Water as an ornamental adjunct to the house has long excited both conventional architects and their landscape counterparts. Ornamental ponds, rills, waterfalls, cascades, fountains, canals, even whole lakes, have long graced the grounds of the great houses of Europe. But we can also see that water around or within the house is universally recognized as bringing an extra dimension to the domestic environment – in the Islamic courtyard and in the

PARIS

compound arrangements of Balinese architecture, where the presence of water, bubbling, running or just standing still, brings an element of peace to buildings and gardens.

Houses, especially those built in relative isolation, have very different relationships to the land around them, cultivated or wild. Some seem to have been simply thrust up with a disregard for their appropriateness in the landscape; others look down from hills and mounds in domination; others hide discreetly behind trees, somehow settled in park or plantation, surrounded perhaps by a garden which is in itself a transition from the land around; others have so many elements of locally available material in their construction that they are scarcely distinguishable from the local terrain. In effect, the successful single house must express, at least in some measure, the spirit of the place in which it stands. Without this, any building outside the larger communities seems curiously at odds with its location and therefore with itself.

Outside the European tradition, houses in Latin America, Africa, south-east Asia and, notably, Mauritius, seem to blend successfully with their location as long as their form and use of materials has been sensitively handled. Long, low houses, with plenty of shade in the form of loggias and verandas, provide a satisfactory respite from days of heat and humidity. Low building, too, has more chance of blending with the landscape, of sheltering behind screens of vegetation; interestingly, our two very grand examples from Goa and Sri Lanka respectively, lie spread across their sites without any of the height of elevation associated with status in temperate climes. Indeed, reflection of local and indigenous cultures and conditions in colour and materials characterizes many of the houses illustrated and helps to give them an air of completeness. Even a low-level habitation in Los Angeles may appropriately symbolize that city's commitment to the modernist design aesthetics of the

GRENOBLE

twentieth century. And a new hotel in Kenya derives its charm and effectiveness from its composition as a series of 'houses' built in the traditional manner with local materials.

What is true of the single house, modest or grand, is also true of the larger communities – village, town and city. Many older concentrations of people and housing presumably grew up largely for defensive or mutually supportive purposes: an enclosure was built for security so that the people of a group could survive and flourish. And

once there was a group of habitations, then all the attendant substructures of services, utilities, governance would fall into place. But even such well-established communities share an inherent contradiction and tension with their newer, planned counterparts: how to balance the privacy of the individual with the intensely public nature of mass building, transport, and commerce?

Many of the illustrations in this chapter of private urban architecture, and town and city living in general, express in some degree the attempts to find an answer to the private/public problem. Streets like those of Bath, Stockholm, parts of London and New York are given a sense of order by a classically-based domestic architecture, behind whose pilasters and architraves the middle classes of the city could retreat to privacy. The high-rise block, born of steel and concrete technology, provides another solution to the housing of large numbers of people in circumstances that guarantee that a reasonable amount of human dignity and individuality can be preserved.

We began the book with a window, albeit a symbolic one. Windows as architectural features can dictate the whole look of a street or square – its line, scale, its feeling of openness or of closure and claustrophobia – as the many examples at the end of the chapter show. At the same time, windows (like doors) are the means by which we can both satisfy our need for privacy, and observe the world outside. Is it raining or sunny? Dawn or dusk? Whether we like it or not, the greyness of a day or the sight of a patch of sunlight on the wall may influence our lives as much as the number of bathrooms, the choice of furniture or the colour of walls.

NICE

Preceding pages
Very few places on the earth's surface are totally devoid of indications of the human imprint. On the plains or in the mountains, there are almost always signs that man has made some attempt to impose himself on the environment, however inhospitable. Other landscapes – that of Tuscany, for example (*p. 27*) – seem to plead for human habitation in their richness and variety; almost any view in that land will take in villages clustered around some hill, rising above vineyards punctuated by the tall forms of cypresses.

Choosing a place to live is frequently a means of expressing how we wish to live, both in work and leisure. This house near Cape Town (*top left*) stands amid its owner's vineyards; a fishing lodge is the very symbol of isolation on the shores of a Scottish loch (*below left*).

The classic landscape of Tuscany and
its classic habitation: a hill-top
farmhouse surrounded by cypress
trees (*top right*); this is a vision
which somehow seems to spring
from a Renaissance painting, one of
those happy instances where man
has created houses, villages and
towns at one with the natural surroundings. Access to leisure facilities
and opportunities may also dictate
choice of lifestyle; these alpine
chalets offer easy access to the ski
slopes of Haute-Savoie, eastern
France (*below right*).

CORSICA

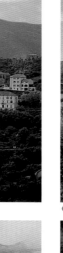

CUBA

CHILOÉ

SCOTLAND

BURUNDI

CHILE

TANGIER

MASSACHUSETTS

CANADA

MEXICO

MASSACHUSETTS

ROMANIA

The places – communities and single habitations – in which we choose to live sit differently in the landscape (*opposite*). Some look so at ease with their immediate topography as seemingly to have grown out of it, like the village in Burundi or the hillside town on the island of Corsica. Others, like the Scottish shooting lodge or the Massachusetts farmhouse, while still using local materials, appear more the result of deliberate building, of an effort to dominate the land around. Farming and husbandry, of course, are foremost in man's effort to make sense of the natural environment; and so in this Welsh agricultural community (*right*), the local herd is moved along the lanes which are in themselves another way of inhabiting nature.

BY THE WATER

Dwellings at the water's edge – by the sea or on the banks of lake or river – hark back to a primitive stage of human occupation of the land. Water provided immediate and abundant food, a means of transport and, in some cases, of defence, although this simple lakeside cottage in Connemara, western Ireland, looks lost and vulnerable against the masses of water and land.

These examples of waterside living and construction (*overleaf*) all have something in common, despite their very different forms and locations: the presence of water dramatizes and enlivens their position on lake, river or sea. Whole towns and cities, such as Venice and Stockholm, are illuminated by the special light which attends closeness to the sea; single houses gain an extra dimension on natural or man-made stretches of water.

SRI LANKA

VENICE LAGOON

CHILOË

MARSEILLES

SANTORINI

IRELAND

BORA-BORA

BURGUNDY

ÎLE DE RÉ

STOCKHOLM

NORWAY

BALI

Light from the sea is unlike light over land: it is more luminous, more vibrant and somehow more pure. The very ordinary architecture of these two communities – one bathed in the colder light of the Scottish coast (*top left*), the other very much under southern skies on the island of Chiloë at the tip of Chile (*below left*) – is transformed into something attractive and engaging.

From the inside looking out; again, the presence of water enlivens and lightens interiors. This terrace of a summer residence in southern Chile (*top right*) gives the illusion of being immediately over the water. Smaller islands, too, are charged with special excitement by the encircling presence of the sea; on the loggia of this villa in Mauritius (*below right*) there is a sense that water is not far away.

A house by the sea or on an island is one solution to the need to escape increasingly crowded and cramped urban centres, to find space and light and also establish a pleasant domestic environment. The owners of this house (*top* and *below left*) on the Île de Ré, off the west coast of France, have sought simplicity in these bright interiors, which clearly benefit from the fresh island light. On another French island, Corsica, the owner of this house (*opposite*) constructs fantastic furniture-sculpture with driftwood.

ON THE LAND

All the houses illustrated here (*these pages* and *overleaf*) have been built in their particular locations as the result of very conscious decisions. Although their siting varies, topographically and climatologically, they all have the air of having been deliberately raised in their individual settings.

Some, indeed, look positively assertive, pitched roofs thrusting upwards, announcing their domination of the land around them. Each one, though, is undeniably stylish in its own way: high ornamental in Sri Lanka (*top left*); suburban villa in Quebec (*below left*); modern minimalist in Belgium (*opposite top*); and Gustavian classicism in Sweden (*opposite below*).

Overleaf
Many of these dwellings are
essentially estate houses, homes of
the owners of the land immediately
around them and possibly of that
much farther afield. All are a
combination of historical, geographical and social factors, from a
broadly based European classicism
in France and Sweden to Islamic
forms in Andalucia, to decorative
elaboration in Thailand.

CHILE

SWEDEN

BURGUNDY

CHILOË

MAURITIUS

HAUTE-SAVOIE

CANADA

MAURITIUS

BURGUNDY

BANGKOK

LOT

ANDALUCIA

DORDOGNE

CANADA

LUCCA

SCOTLAND

CANADA

SRI LANKA

Grand houses, whether in the town or the country, have traditionally provided security and comfort. As the need for the former declined, so the attention paid to the latter increased, finding one of its finest expressions in the decoration of the great Italian palaces of the Renaissance and Baroque periods: here, all the accoutrements of gracious living in the summer palace of the Chigi family, Rome (*right*).

The estate houses in former European colonies frequently show interesting mixtures of styles: Indo-Portuguese in Goa (*top left*), and English Suburban in Sri Lanka (*below left*). In its elaborately styled façades, embellished with multiple balconies, this privately owned Goan palace has a grandeur which is entirely Iberian, a reflection of the sumptuous lifestyle of the family for whom it was built in the eighteenth century.

Inside the Bragança Palace in Goa (*top* and *below right*) gallery leads to gallery via open-work doors of carved wood. The magnificent ballroom, seen here, was redecorated during the nineteenth century; its floor is covered in Italian marble, reflecting the light from the Belgian chandeliers. More light floods through the arched windows of the whole *piano nobile*.

When natural building materials are immediately available and plentiful, local housing really does seem to take on the forms and colours of the surrounding vegetation and of the land from which it grows. In Tahiti, paradise island of Gauguin, this waterside house (*top left*) is scarcely distinguishable from the dense plant life that surrounds it. A compound in Kenya (*below left*) has the same quality of seeming to grow from the ground it stands on, the roof forming a canopy like that of trees in a forest. New building regulations for such locations stipulate that houses should be no higher than a palm tree.

In recognition, perhaps, of the common-sense of building in local materials, a number of hotel chains around the world have begun to make this a feature of new constructions. Such developments are also a recognition that local and indigenous cultures are important and to be respected. This hotel (*top* and *below right*), at Kurayu in Kenya, close to that country's northern border with Somalia, is made up of twenty separate 'houses', thus granting independence to the guests but still retaining the luxury of hotel services. Each separate residential entity is built from woven palm leaves in the traditional manner of the region. Inside, the local themes are continued in the furnishing, but with a distinctly luxurious interpretation.

Overleaf
An entirely private residence built in local materials is this house on the Indonesian island of Sumbawa, east of Bali and Lombok. As the contents of this splendid space suggest, it belongs to an artist who works principally in wood, sculpting marvellous and strange articles of furniture. In this, he has taken up the traditions of the local community, makers of dugout canoes out of solid wood.

SAN FRANCISCO

CARIBBEAN

CHILOÉ

MAURITIUS

NEPAL

CAIRO

FLORIDA

SCOTLAND

BANGKOK

SLOVAKIA

LOS ANGELES

BURUNDI

53

SALZBURG

MAURITIUS

SAN FRANCISCO

MAURITIUS

MAURITIUS

IRELAND

CANADA

MAURITIUS

THAILAND

CHILE

BALI

CHILOË

Preceding pages
Modernist one-storey in Los Angeles, Normandy-style villa in Mauritius, or Islamic enclosure in Cairo, all these houses suggest life on the edge of towns, somewhere at the point where the rural meets the urban. They are, effectively, in their very different ways, examples of the villa, neither country estate house nor yet townhouse.

Even though many of the houses illustrated here (*opposite*) are effectively in towns – for instance, the 1894 villas of the San Francisco hills ('painted ladies') or elegant Irish Georgian – most still retain a certain sense of scale; they do not yet suggest the intensity of the city life of apartments and narrow-fronted townhouses. Paradoxically, however, the façade of this house in the Massachusetts model village of Sturbridge does have a distinct look of its antecedents in English and Dutch towns (*top right*), while having the same proportions as a very urban block in Luxor, Egypt (*below right*).

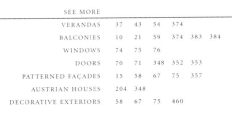

STOCKHOLM

MANHATTAN

STOCKHOLM

NICE

BATH

MANHATTAN

IN TOWN AND CITY

One practical and elegant solution to the problems of living with privacy in large conurbations is the townhouse (*opposite*). The 'brownstones' of Manhattan, with their characteristic sandstone façades and 'stoops', and their cousins in England, Ireland and northern Europe, provided comfortable urban living for the burgeoning middle and merchant classes of the nineteenth century. However, pressure of demand for accommodation has led to the conversion of the majority of them into apartment houses to provide the same kind of living as the high-rise blocks of larger European and American cities.

The 'main street' is repeated endlessly in different forms all over the world, from Brazil (*top right*) to Ireland (*below right*): the one street in town or in the neighbourhood where people meet, shop, gossip, sit in bars. In northern climates actual street life tends to be less vigorously pursued than in southern climates with Latin traditions. Sadly, these centres of community life are now under threat as activity transfers to edge-of-town malls.

The form of the tower has become the modern city's answer to the problem of masses of people congregating in cities to live and work. While the post-office (*opposite*) at Trivandrum, Kerala, India may not be compared in function to a modern apartment block in Cairo (*right*), the juxtaposition does emphasize the way in which cityscapes the world over have become very much more vertical at the expense of the lateral, a verticality largely made possible by the advent of reinforced concrete.

Concentrations of population demand to be housed. Where communities grow up without planning, their habitations, too, seem to cling together in some strange organic fashion, like this cluster of houses and churches on the Greek island of Santorini (*top left*). Classical order and planning, in contrast, are guiding principles in the city of Bath, a place of stylish terraces and townhouses (*below left*).

Like the Santorini hill villages, the homes of the mountain Berbers in the Dra valley of Morocco (*top right*) seem simply to have grown into place and look entirely at one with the local rock. They also show that large numbers of humans had found it possible to live together long before the flat roofs of the apartment blocks and industrial buildings of Manhattan (*below right*) were raised to their lofty position.

A snow-bound street in Quebec looks all the friendlier for the relative absence of motorized traffic (*left*). The closeness of the housing expresses a sense of community, reinforced by the sight of pedestrians in the street.

The presence of large numbers of pedestrians enlivens the urban environment. What happens spontaneously and naturally in a town of colour and celebration like Lucban on the island of Luzon in the Philippines (*right*) is now part of local government legislation in many towns and cities of the Western world: the introduction of pedestrianized zones.

An essential part of any community's life, providing havens of peace and places for reflection, are its chapels, churches and temples. Their interiors, too, are usually immediately expressive of how a community approaches its engagement with religious practice and belief, of how it worships. A small church in Atacama, southern Chile, is still full of imagery and decorative elements (*top left*). A spartan Methodist chapel in a Welsh village (*below left*) has a simplicity in keeping with the underlying puritanism of that particular interpretation of Christianity.

Whatever belief or creed a community subscribes to, buildings devoted to worship provide relief from the material, sometimes painful concerns of the world without. The styles in which they are decorated are a means of celebration for their congregations, whose own homes may be in strict contrast to the opulence of the altars and chapels illustrated here: in Chile (*top* and *below left*) and in a Goan palace (*below right*).

Overleaf
The public face of churches and temples usually confirms their status as being among the most important buildings in village, town and city, demanding lavish attention and care, dominating surrounding dwellings by their height and architectural magnificence.

COCHIN

SANTORINI

MEXICO

CHILOË

MEXICO

CHILOË

ROMANIA

MANILA

COCHIN

MEXICO

ST. PETERSBURG

MEXICO

GUATEMALA >

SHANGHAI

CHILE

MEXICO

SCOTLAND

TUNIS

COPENHAGEN

MAURITIUS

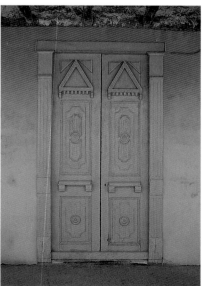

IRELAND

CHILE

CHILOË

CHILOË

CHILE

Preceding pages

Urban planning in the West reached a kind of perfection in the development and refinement of the townhouse. There are few sights more satisfying to the lover of order in the city than that of a row of New York 'brownstones', or of nineteenth-century English or Dutch terraces. In the case of the 'brownstones', the door – always an important feature – is given enhanced importance by the massive 'stoop' leading to it from the pavement.

As the means of transition from the public world of the street to the privacy of the interior the outside door of access has been recognized by most cultures as worthy of intense design attention and decoration (*these pages*). From the public statements of good proportions and order in Irish Georgian to the suggestion of secret things within the enclosure guarded by a massive portal in Tunis, all these doors tell us something about the building for which they are the means of entry.

ST. PETERSBURG

HELSINKI

HELSINKI

NORWAY

SALZBURG

LUXOR

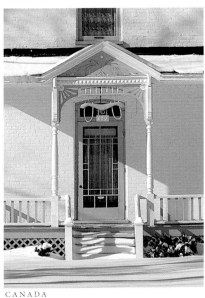

CANADA

IRELAND

CHILE

SANTIAGO

NICE

BUDAPEST

NICE

SEVILLE

UMBRIA

NAPLES

SHANGHAI

SALVADOR DI BAHIA

CHILOÉ

SWEDEN

LUXOR

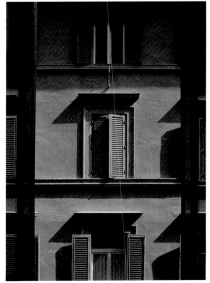

ROME

PORTO

HAUTE-SAVOIE

CHILOÉ

MANHATTAN

PORTO

NEPAL

BANGKOK

PROVENCE

BOMBAY

ISTANBUL

ISTANBUL

BATH

NAPLES

CHILE

NEPAL

PORTO

NICE

MAURITIUS

VIENNA

CHILOÉ

MARRAKESH

BUDAPEST

PALERMO

NEPAL >

GOA

GOA

NICE

MEXICO

ARGENTINA

PARIS

WINDOWS ON THE WORLD

Like doors, windows are agents of transition between public and private. Looking out from them, we can observe our surroundings from a vantage point; in turn, they allow the outside into our living and working spaces in the form of light and air. Again, like doors, they are important details in the overall design of buildings, set within elaborate surrounds or taking surprising shapes. Sometimes their forms are strictly utilitarian, like those in these traditional dwellings in Bangkok (*pp. 72–73*), set amid materials of such rough texture that the structures themselves suggest the very activity of building, or the window in a Nepalese house, surrounded by drying maize (*p. 77*).

On the inside looking out, windows may be major features in any interior decoration scheme (*these pages*), enhanced by curtains or elaborately patterned blinds and shutters, partly veiled or open to reveal some pleasing vista, or providing the ideal position for a favourite chair.

IBIZA

Windows always act as framing devices, as we look out to the great beyond or to the other side of a city courtyard: agricultural peace in Wales (*left*), or a secret corner of Havana (*opposite*). In both cases, we seem to have been given access to other, mysterious worlds.

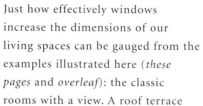

Just how effectively windows increase the dimensions of our living spaces can be gauged from the examples illustrated here (*these pages* and *overleaf*): the classic rooms with a view. A roof terrace provides a further extension to a French window in a Corsican house (*above left*); from the windows of the main house on a Massachusetts model farm the working buildings can be observed (*above right*).

This long balconied window of a Paris apartment gives on to the sumptuous architecture of the Place des Vosges beyond (*above left*); beyond an open door lie the varied colours of an English cottage garden at Charleston in Sussex (*above right*). In both cases, the division of the door-windows into smaller panes of glass emphasizes the sense of the inside looking on the outside.

BANGKOK

SHANGHAI

ÎLE DE RÉ

CORSICA

PARIS

CORSICA

BANGKOK

PROVENCE

PROVENCE

PROVENCE

IRELAND

PARIS

DESIGNING FOR LIVING

Inside the home

IN A MODERNIST STYLE

TRADITIONAL SIMPLICITY

COLONIAL INFLUENCES

IN GRACIOUS AND GRAND STYLES

STYLES FOR COMFORT

INDIVIDUAL TOUCHES

INHERITED TEXTURES

A NEW ECLECTICISM

SURVEYING THE DEVASTATION and destruction visited on Italy by the events of the Second World War, the scholar and art critic Mario Praz wrote, 'The houses will rise again, and men will furnish houses as long as there is breath in them. Just as our primitive ancestor built a shapeless chair with hastily-chopped branches, so the last man will save from the rubble a stool or a tree stump on which to rest from his labours; and if his spirit is freed for a while from his woes, he will linger another moment and decorate his room'. Praz's own interest in interior decoration eventually led him to assemble a remarkable collection of original paintings of interiors of all ages, which he eventually published as *An Illustrated History of Interior Decoration*. His sentiments about man's need to embellish the interiors of his habitat will find many echoes in the pages which follow, for all the domestic and some of the public spaces illustrated here are very much direct extensions of the lives of the people who designed them and who, in many cases, still live in them.

This sequence of illustrations is not historical, nor do they relate in any way to strictly defined styles. In fact, what is especially engaging about many of the rooms here is the eclecticism in arrangement and furnishing that informs their appearance, sometimes to the extent of making a positive virtue out of clutter and the deliberate juxtaposition of apparently incongruous artefacts. Yet, in the larger sense, humble or grand, they are all stylish, whether coated with the patinas of long occupation or the fresh expression of the home-maker's latest vision. If any central theme emerges from the images, it is that of addition and accretion; we begin with relatively spare, purist designs and then progress by various degrees of more or less self-conscious embellishment, to the straightforward search for comfort, and end with rooms where pure, formal arrangement of apparently disparate elements is the guiding principle.

A modernist aesthetic can be applied in various circumstances; it doesn't necessarily emerge only in contemporary or near-contemporary buildings and designs. A way of arranging furniture can be modernist, even though it is in the context of a seventeenth-century apartment, where it can be even more effective. One of the more uncompromisingly pure modern interiors illustrated is in fact in a converted London Victorian house. Another development of such an aesthetic is a relative lack of free-standing furniture, thus obliging us to take more notice of surfaces – walls and floors – and of interconnecting devices like staircases. There is still an eclectic excitement here, however, notably in the cross-fertilization of styles; thus, Oriental and Scandinavian influences come together in a contemporary English interior. In the United States, especially in Los Angeles and Chicago, many of the theories and practices of design developed at the Bauhaus and loosely grouped under the term 'International Modernism' found their most complete expression, often in the work of European *émigrés*.

The spare elegance of the modernist interior can easily inform more traditional settings, especially when the furniture and decor are of very fine quality. The period and the style of the interiors may vary, but there is a kind of traditional good taste that surmounts national, regional and

NEW YORK

cultural differences. We may find the same spirit in the pared-down reserve of a Manhattan apartment, in the cool interiors of a Marrakesh house, or even behind the restored vaulted stone walls of Mediterranean dwellings in Provence and Mallorca.

There is usually a certain homogeneity in the furnishings and decors of such homes. From this point onward, however, we begin to look at eclecticism in the interior, first from a personal aspect and then from the point of view of intermingling cultures. We now see the use of furniture of varying styles, perhaps mixing inexpensive but classic items from furniture chain stores with older, rustic pieces. Personal objects begin to take on prominence, reflecting sporting or cultural interests. Kitchens and the other working rooms of the house provide valuable opportunities

for mixing utensils as well as more conventional ornament; there is now a recognition that the equipment of the kitchen can be attractive in its own right and therefore worthy of display. Studies and book-rooms, too, can become highly personalized spaces for the arrangement of objects, squeezed between books or placed in front of them, which might look out of place in the formality of a drawing-room or dining-room.

Influences from other cultures make for especially exciting possibilities. We have included many examples of Oriental styles, minimalist and highly decorative; both extremes are instructive for the home decorator. Minimalism in the handling of the volume and scale of some of the interiors has contributed to western modernism, as witness some of the schemes illustrated in the early part of this chapter. Decorative furniture – cabinets, chests in lacquer-work – can look effective anywhere in the world; they can also strike a marvellously exotic note in apartments in, say, London, Paris and New York. We respond to the messages they bring and the history and cultures they evoke – particularly when seen outside their own context.

FINLAND

What we have termed 'Colonial Influences' covers a number of strikingly beautiful interiors that derive much of their interest from the meeting of distinct cultures: Hispanic with Latin American and Filipino, English with Sri Lankan and, in one remarkable Goan palace that has been in the possession of the same family for nearly three hundred years, Portuguese and Indian.

Some of the interiors illustrated in these pages are very

grand indeed, notably those within *palazzi* in Rome and Sicily, where the decorators of the Baroque and Rococo periods indulged their wildest fantasies in the creation of sumptuously painted rooms and voluptuously curving plasterwork. Of course, such places were exclusively the domain of the aristocracy and rich merchant classes. When the burgeoning middle classes of western Europe and North America wished to give outward expression to their growing financial power, they too wanted a version of traditional luxury, with the trappings of wealth – libraries, paintings, trophies; hence, we have the heavily furnished, heavily patterned interiors of the Victorian era, which can be found

PARIS

as far apart as Sicily and Quebec. Cultural and geographical differences, however, can be quite distinctive; there is, for instance, an entirely northern economy and restraint in the many Scandinavian and Scottish interiors illustrated here. But there is one remarkable example of cultural crossover in a Finnish country house decorated in varying interpretations of southern Baroque and Rococo.

Comfort is classless; each person searches for it according to his or her means. It is warmth and shelter; it is the accommodation of the family, sometimes extended; it is flexibility – allowing for winter and summer, for heat and cold, for children to grow up; it is also the freedom to enjoy the company of friends, of prized and loved possessions, to project an atmosphere of one's own making within the walls of the home. From the humble miner's cottage, from log cabin (both examples now preserved as folk-museums, now an important source for our knowledge of the past domestic environment) to metropolitan apartments stuffed with the

books, paintings and ornaments of vigorously cultural urban lives, the search for a welcoming, personalized environment is a powerful force indeed. This projection of the individual through decor can take many forms: the display of personal effects, of collections (ranging from ceramics to sumptuous fabrics), the theming of rooms, or even the adoption of a *laissez-faire* attitude towards decoration, entailing minimum intervention in what is already there. Thus, walls may be left untreated, floor boards unpolished and plasterwork and painting incomplete.

Collecting can be seen as another stage in the process of creating a specific atmosphere; the formal arrangements and displays illustrated in the final pages of this chapter are the visible statements of a wish on the part of the home-makers to live in a very particular and individual way. But although there is a unifying spirit of formality in the cabinets, kitchens, sitting-rooms and bedrooms in places as diverse as Provence, Paris, New York and Milan, not one of the

SAN FRANCISCO

arrangements has the dead air of a museum; all of them still resonate with the spirit of the person or persons who created them.

Finally, we concur, with Mario Praz, on the fascination these varied expressions of the decorative impulse hold for us, '...beautiful were the richly-decorated salons of your palaces, the calm rooms of your old bourgeois houses, the rustic kitchens of your simple dwellings in the mountains; beautiful also was your furniture with its time-stained patina, your objects lovingly worked by generations of cabinet-makers, potters and goldsmiths!'.

IN A MODERNIST STYLE

These two apartments (*preceding pages* and *these pages*) express an essentially modernist aesthetic by careful juxtaposition of setting and objects. In the first, the generous spaces of a seventeenth-century Paris apartment have been stripped to their essentials to house a collection of twentieth-century furniture classics. The chairs and tables, though of very different date from that of the huge sitting-room, do not in any way seem at odds with it; but, then, the lines of the pieces by Jean Prouvé, Charlotte Perriand and Harry Bertoia are also expressive of a new classicism.

In contrast, the apartment illustrated here (*these pages*), which belongs to a Parisian interior designer, has an entirely contemporary feel to its rooms, but the artefacts it contains are self-consciously decorative: an elaborately branched chandelier, looking-glasses within Rococo frames, and a button-back settee. Storage shelves are concealed by the voluminous curtains which are drawn by means of long bamboo poles.

Behind the traditional façade of a London house lies this interior (*above*), cool and minimalist, seemingly Scandinavian and Oriental in inspiration. The orderly lines of the design start, literally, at floor level with wide boards of Oregon pine. All the decorative elements of the original Victorian interior have been suppressed and the interior walls removed; only two vestiges remain in the form of the open fireplaces, given horizontal proportions to accentuate the length of the room and simplified to their bare, functional essentials. All the clutter which could detract from the strength of the rectilinear design is safely concealed in capacious floor-to-ceiling cupboards.

One gesture towards a more flamboyant approach to decoration in this otherwise simple Mallorcan interior (*above*) is the Ottoman star form of the ceiling lights. Otherwise, everything is simplification itself, from the director chairs to the ingenious creation of a fireplace by inserting a second wall to form the chimney-breast.

The disposition of furniture in this San Francisco apartment (*top* and *below left*) makes a feature of the windows as points of focus. Such a loose and fluid use of space is entirely appropriate to contemporary apartment living, where rooms have often been stripped of all traditional features.

The effect of total, stripped-down modernism is very similar in both these houses. Their difference lies in the fact that one (*top right*) is a masterly, transforming conversion within the shell of a traditional London Victorian house, while the other is part of a totally conceived and realized modernist construction by Richard Neutra in Los Angeles (*below right*). Indeed, Neutra's own brand of International Modernism very much shaped the design vision of that city from the 1930s to the 1960s in its promotion of cool, logically managed environments – the Californian interpretation of the European work of Gropius and Le Corbusier.

The successful management of space is the key to making most modernist interiors work. A relative absence of free-standing furniture concentrates attention on walls, floors and connecting elements like staircases and openings. Within the converted London house (*p. 97*) the kitchen area and bedrooms connect with other parts of the house by open square arches (*top far left* and *below right*). The influence of Japanese minimalism is plainly evident in the bedroom arrangement. Ingenious and dramatic use of adjoining spaces characterize this Brussels interior: a staircase leading to a light, uncluttered bedroom which, in turn, gives on to a roof terrace covered in teak decking (*top right*).

Living in converted industrial premises is often associated with New York and the fashion of loft dwelling; however, this converted print factory is in Paris (*below far left* and *opposite*). In keeping with the building's origins, the bathroom makes use of industrial elements – a clothes rack for towels and heavy-duty glass blocks concealing a light source. White cotton drapes soften the lines of the mezzanine reading area (*opposite*); a further counter to the straight lines of the main layout is provided by the curvilinear organic-modernist 'Butterfly' chair, originally designed in the late 1930s, and the splendid sweeping form of 'La Chaise', by Charles Eames, a prototype in 1948.

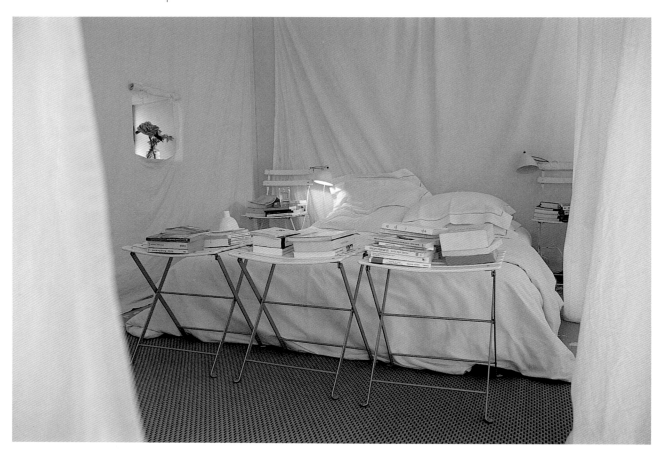

The strict lines and colour schemes of modernist interiors can be successfully countered and also enhanced by the introduction of softer forms and materials into the decorative scheme. The interiors illustrated here (*top* and *below left*), in Paris and London, have the rigour of contemporary minimalism, yet both of them are made more attractive by the presence of textiles and other isolated elements: voluminous bed coverings; the contours of a large duvet; a vase of flowers. In the Paris apartment the whole room has a 'soft' quality much enhanced by the tent-like hanging of white cotton drapes.

In these two interiors – in Paris (*top right*) and Mallorca (*below right*) – a number of elements have been introduced which mitigate what would otherwise be a very spartan effect. A large artwork, with strong graphic motifs, dominates this mezzanine area. The Mallorcan summer house, the home of a rug and carpet designer, though of relatively recent construction, still manages to reflect tradition in exposed beams and sloping ceilings. Strongly shaped free-standing objects and flowers provide other points of focus.

DEVON

All the bathrooms illustrated here are utilitarian (*these pages*); they are also beautiful and exciting spaces, a reflection of this room's modern status as a place for serious design focus. Though eschewing all additional decoration, the quality of the materials and the style of the fittings make these spaces ones in which to linger. Again, the presence of a folded towel, wall photograph or vase of flowers sets off hard surfaces of zinc, stainless steel and white ceramic.

CARPENTRAS

PARIS

CARPENTRAS

LONDON

PARIS

MALLORCA

PARIS

A modernist aesthetic does not necessarily mean that design should be dull. The shapes of the fittings in a London house (*above*) are intriguing in themselves, though they have the clean lines of a purist approach to decoration. The baths are interpretations of traditional Japanese forms; the shower room is a complete, integrated environment, where water simply drains away through outlets in the floor.

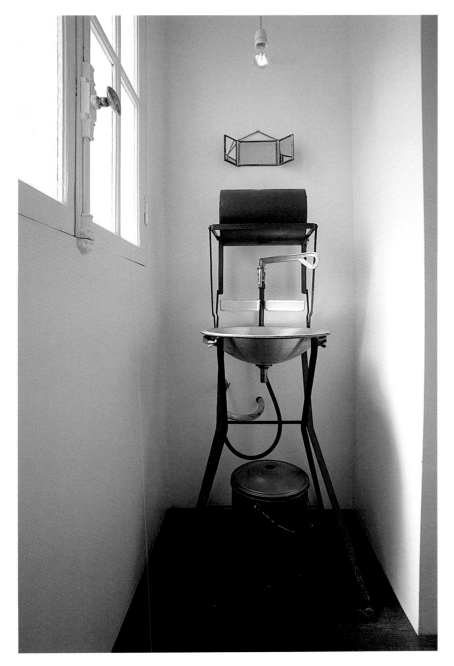 

Taking a somewhat different approach to introducing fantasy into otherwise very simply conceived bathrooms, the owners of these two Paris interiors (*above*) have chosen to enliven small spaces by installing highly decorative fittings. These look all the more dramatic for being in all-white settings, and have a truly surreal look, arising from the juxtaposition of disparate objects and their apparent incongruity here.

Though still clearly contemporary in colour and form, the bathrooms illustrated here are distinctly places of pleasure. Materials and decorative additions announce them as environments in which the senses are to be satisfied. Carefully placed ornaments provide an elegant distraction in Marrakesh (*top left*). And one certain way to lend notes of interest to any bathroom is to make a small display of bottles of scent and waters (*below left*).

An even greater sense of sybaritic
luxury pervades this Italian
bathroom (*top right*), with walls
hung with framed engravings. In
this Moorish bathroom (*below right*)
walls and bath are coated in a
traditional chalk-based plaster.

Modernist kitchens can sometimes have a distinctly industrial look; this example in a Brussels apartment, for instance, is dominated by neat linear units and an extractor vent (*opposite*). This somewhat spartan effect can be softened by the open display of kitchen utensils in all their variety of form and colour. The number of objects and equipment displayed in this Paris kitchen (*top right*) indicates that this is a place devoted to serious food preparation. Another Paris apartment (*below right*) uses open semi-industrial units for storage, but achieves a distinctly lived-in effect through the visible accumulations of crockery and utensils.

Finding ways of linking eating areas with other parts of the house, either kitchens or sitting-rooms, calls for some design ingenuity. The introduction of open storage units can sometimes provide the solution. This striking blue dresser in a Sicilian kitchen immediately extends the room's decorative possibilities (*above left*). In this Paris apartment (*below left*), two metal support pillars have been inserted to open up the wall between the sitting-room and the dining area, thus fully displaying the immense 'Trapèze' table and the 'Standard' chairs designed by Jean Prouvé. As a fashion, Hi-Tech moved to the centre of the decorative arts and interior design in the 1970s; it was characterized by the use of heavy-duty industrial artefacts and equipment in domestic contexts. This dining area of a Provençal house picks up resonances of the style with mass-produced steel chairs and an industrial refrigerator unit mounted on wheels (*opposite*).

Simple lines and simple shapes are just as effective as displays of opulence in creating attractive living quarters. Indeed, the elegance of the finest Oriental design has often been the inspiration for western modernist architects and designers. However, the creator of the house (*above left*) in Tokyo, the potter Shoji Hamada, was influenced in his work by a westerner, the Englishman Bernard Leach, another advocate of uncluttered, earthy form in the decorative arts. The rooms in this Carpentras house (*above right*) are connected by archways with open-work screens of Japanese inspiration.

These two interiors, one in New York (*above left*) and one in Paris (*above right*) exude elegant modernism in their distribution of furniture in simple, tidy groupings. Yet, the forms of the chairs and sofa also suggest a more old-fashioned concern with comfort. The elegant chic of the Paris interior is entirely in keeping with the spirit and ideals of the organization to which it belongs, the house of Chanel.

It would be reasonable to expect an apartment in Manhattan to exhibit some of the qualities of New York's devotion to change and progress in the nineteenth and twentieth centuries. And there is indeed a straightforwardness and modernity in the arrangement of furniture in these two rooms (*these pages*). Effects of lightness and spaciousness are enhanced by the presence of the large mirrors above the fireplaces and two sumptuous Fortuny lights.

The furniture is largely early-nineteenth-century; one particularly interesting piece is an Empire Style day-bed, with characteristic scroll ends. American furniture of the period was much influenced by French fashions, several French firms of cabinet-makers having established themselves in New York during the period as an escape from the political instability of Europe.

TRADITIONAL SIMPLICITY

Traditional vaulted ceilings, especially if quite low, create a sense of intimacy and containment, ideal for a dining area or place where people can engage in intimate conversation. The roughly hewn stonework of an Apulian house provides an ideal setting, giving on to a courtyard, for eating outside (*above left*). The more formal interior dining-room in the same house (*above right*) takes up the shape again in a much more finished form, although it was in fact converted from a former stable.

In the same Italian house (*above right*) a more relaxed sitting area occupies the interesting spaces created by the relationship of several arches and a vaulted ceiling. As an architectural form the arch is of great significance in the Islamic world, since it suggests the prayer alcove, the mihrab, repeated on every traditional prayer rug. This

example, a conversation corner (used also as the winter dining-room) in a Marrakesh house (*above left*), is decorated with finely detailed polychrome decoration. The walls are covered to mid-height with padded canvas, decorated with motifs taken from desert Arab tents. The design of the chairs is derived from traditional Moroccan forms.

In the old stone houses of the whole Mediterranean region the rounded arch and vaulted ceiling are traditional forms, usually built in rugged local stone which, when cleaned, is a decorative element in itself. Underneath the majestic curving vault of this former stable of a house in Mallorca (*above*) the owners have installed a bath-house. One of the only features to have been completely renewed is the floor, now a mosaic of blue *pâte-de-verre*.

A vaulted room in this Provençal *mas*, home to a French interior designer, makes a light and airy bedroom (*above*). The rough-cast wall surface has been cleaned but still lends a rugged charm to the whole ensemble. The floor is composed of traditional Provençal terracotta tiles. The arch is echoed in the forms of door and window, but the angled bed form has been chosen to contrast with it.

Overleaf
Again, the vaulted form is visible in the dining area of the house in Mallorca, where more recent additions have the material strength and forthrightness of the original structure. A chimney has been created on one side of the area to provide a vent for the table-height grill; beneath it is a rectangular cavity for storing logs.

All the bedrooms illustrated here demonstrate one fundamental design principle: how the strong traditional lines of an original building and its interiors can be set off by the judicious arrangement of interesting personal objects and soft furnishings. An arch provides a convenient niche for the bed-head (*top far left*) in this Paris apartment and an opportunity to hang part of the owner's collection of paintings and photographs by contemporary artists. More personal clutter is stacked on the bedside chest of drawers. In this Marrakesh bedroom (*top left*) the bed and the matching armchair are strong decorative elements in themselves. Light textiles, either in hanging form or as bed linen, enliven these two bedrooms – one, French (*below far left*), and one, Sicilian (*below left*). Even this somewhat monkish, cell-like guest bedroom in a Provençal house (*opposite*) has been personalized by the addition of traditional terracotta jars to serve both utilitarian and ornamental purposes.

Simplicity of structure and decoration are somehow utterly appropriate in houses in warmer climates. Both this bedroom (*above*) and this children's dormitory (*opposite*) are in a Provençal house.

Both exhibit a straightforward
attitude to construction and
decoration. But the addition of any
decorative element, such as an
Oriental rug, has an instantly
dramatic effect.

Inviting, with the promise of easy, intimate conversation, yet also relaxing in its combination of whites and greys, this bed-sitting-room in a Marrakesh *riad* beautifully combines the traditional and the new. The simple, direct forms of the chairs and fireplace are a perfect foil for the rich textures of the heavy curtains (protection from the sunlight during the day and from the cold at night) and, on the floor, a traditional Tuareg rug in woven straw and leather. Invisible here is another feature: the ceiling is in the form of an upturned boat.

The interiors illustrated on the pages that follow have been chosen because they incorporate very distinctive and often very personal elements in their decorative schemes, but often from very different sources. Emphasis here is very much on the contents of rooms, sometimes simple, sometimes complex, sometimes exotic, sometimes eclectic, but always fascinating and inspirational. Multiple shifts in wall and ceiling surfaces make this Marrakesh bedroom (*above*) a place of subtle complexities – a suitable setting for furniture whose sturdiness is countered by the delicate decorative touch of the three hanging lamps in a traditional Moroccan design.

This room in a Provençal house (*above*), the holiday home of a fashion designer, painted plainly in white, with exposed beams, is made warm and inviting by the addition of a number of carefully chosen articles of low-level furniture, including two North African *tabourets*, used as occasional tables. Splashes of dramatic colour enliven but never overwhelm the whole setting; large floor candles provide alternative points of focus to the briskly ascending flames of the fire.

These two interior spaces (*top left* and *below left*) in the same house in Carpentras, Provence, show how an eclectic approach to acquiring furniture and objects can result in an entirely pleasing yet workmanlike domestic environment. Much of the furniture has been made to the owner's designs in relatively inexpensive materials. Other items have either been recovered from salvage shops, like the 1940s architect's lamp, or bought from household goods chain-stores.

The house in Marrakesh, already illustrated (*pp. 126–128*), contains several rooms on a smaller scale that the owners have brought to life by the careful positioning of small objects, including traditional hats, and single items of furniture (*top right* and *top far right* and *below right*). One feature common to all is the use of traditional hanging lamps, with their distinctive lines and strong graphic patterning. In a Corsican house, potentially 'dead' space (*below far right*) has been saved by decorative ingenuity in the placing there of two huge flexible baskets and the continuation of the lower wall colour on to the window frame.

Overleaf
A similar attention to detail is evident in all the interior spaces illustrated here. Sometimes it is the transitional space – the stairwell, the corridor, the landing – which requires the most attention in terms of ornament or colour, rather than the grander proportions of principal rooms. But even in the latter it is often important to create corners of interest away from the main axis of attention. These spaces all use pale background colour punctuated by bursts of deeper, brighter hues.

PROVENCE

IBIZA

IBIZA

SICILY

SICILY

PARIS

PROVENCE

MANHATTAN

TUNISIA

NICE

MARRAKESH

PARIS

CÉVENNES

ITALY

NAPLES

CORSICA

PARIS

BALI

PROVENCE

PARIS

MARRAKESH

IRELAND

SAIGON

TUNISIA

Successful decorative effects are not always achieved by the display of intrinsically interesting objects or items of furniture. Personal whimsy can often be turned to effective ornamental use; in this house on the Île de Ré, western France, the owner's sporting interests have delivered him a ready-made wall frieze. The furniture is an eclectic mixture of the formal and the casual, though the placement is very deliberate.

ÎLE DE RÉ

For the creation of a homely yet functional eating area, classic furniture bought from popular stores, such as Habitat and Ikea, can be as effective as more expensive items. Mixed with older pieces, still to be found relatively cheaply in bric-à-brac emporiums, it can create the feeling of warmth and informality which the kitchen-dining-rooms illustrated on these pages exude. Only the minimalist Parisian dining-room (*opposite below far right*) attracts by the sculptural form of a single article of furniture.

ÎLE DE RÉ

ÎLE DE RÉ

SEVILLE

MALLORCA

SICILY

PROVENCE

PARIS

The circumstances of modern urban living often re-emphasize the central role of the kitchen in our culture; for reasons of space, this is the place where many of us choose to eat and where food can be served directly from the utensils of its preparation. There is, then, good reason to make sure that the kitchen is made attractive by displays of crockery, fruit or flowers, as in this example in San Francisco (*top left*), and in a more rustic version in Mallorca (*below left*).

We expect to be looked after in the kitchen; the combination of heat and sustenance there recalls a distant ancestor, the communal cooking fire. It is associated with stir, bustle, warmth, richness and ripeness. It is the one room which drives the apartment or house in which it is located. So, this very friendliness makes it an ideal place for self-indulgence in decorative detail, in the display of objects of interesting shape but of no particular value, like this arrangement of bowls and teapots in an Irish kitchen (*below right*); even the refrigerator offers opportunities for embellishment. Kitchen utensils themselves, especially polished pans and baskets, combined with herbs or fruit, can make very engaging displays – here, in a kitchen of a house on the island of Ibiza (*top right*).

This magnificent kitchen in a house in Santiago, Chile, is clearly intended as a serious temple of the culinary arts (*opposite* and *top right* and *far right*). All the actual cooking facilities are located centrally under the powerful and sculptural abstract form of the extractor vent. It is worth noting, though, that the table also occupies a position of prominence, reminding us of the importance of this flat surface in the kitchen environment, as an area for food preparation and for eating. After all, who needs a dining-room if the kitchen table is large and accommodating? It draws groups and families together and associates them with both the preparation and consumption of food. Both these examples (*below right* and *far right*) – one in Buenos Aires, and the other the kitchen-like corner of a *salon* in a house on the Île de Ré, western France – are attractive enough; the latter's decoration includes kitchen items and objects reflecting the owner's nautical interests.

COLONIAL INFLUENCES

The quality of light flooding through the windows of these two interiors – a New York loft (*top left*) and a palace bedroom in Goa (*below left*) – gives both of them a look of being elevated above the more earthly concerns of ground-floor living. The apartment in New York is in fact in the city's SoHo district, where an abundance of warehouse and light industrial premises became available for conversion in the 1970s, as businesses relocated to the suburbs, thus initiating the fashion for loft living. Of quite different provenance, the grand scale of this palace in Goa (*below left*) was intended to reflect the lavish lifestyle of one of the grand families of the former Portuguese colony. The same opulence is abundantly expressed in the furniture of the palace – like this four-poster bed hung with lacework – a strange cross of Iberian and Goan styles.

This first-floor sitting-room of a house in Versailles (*right*) is also furnished largely in a mixture of European and Indian styles and materials. Around a black lacquer table, on which is displayed a collection of 1930s bronzes by Christofle, are grouped a number of Anglo-Indian armchairs in carved ebony, a chest of similar provenance in mahogany and ivory and a seventeenth-century cabinet in ebony. The whole grouping is illuminated by the special quality of light that floods through the first-floor windows.

The Spanish and Portuguese taste for lavishly carved furniture reappears in houses in many parts of the world: a *salon* in Havana (*above left*); rooms in the Bragança Palace, Goa (*above right* and *opposite*). Carved in rosewood by local craftsmen, the design of the chairs and tables in the palace is eighteenth-century Portuguese.

Although very clear decorative impulses have been brought to bear on the rooms of this Sri Lankan house (*left*) in the form of carved doorways and furniture, the overall effect is one of graceful simplicity. Also decorative, but with the clutter and memorabilia, the accretions of continuous occupancy by generations of the same family since the eighteenth century, the galleries of the Bragança Palace in Goa are a treasure house of Indo-European design (*opposite*).

The generously proportioned galleries of the Closenberg Hotel, an old-style colonial building in Galle, Sri Lanka (*these pages*), are made luminous by the natural light filtered by huge arched windows. Disposed throughout all the rooms is a magnificent assembly of antique furniture made by local craftsmen, ranging from the sobriety of traditional planters' chairs to highly ornate re-interpretations of indigenous and European styles.

Domestic architecture of the far Orient has much to teach the West in the use and articulation of spatial volumes. Low roofs and ceilings limit the amount of bright light entering the extensive sitting areas in a house in Manila (*top left*) and in this Balinese residence (*below left*). Low furniture, often made of local hardwoods, is distributed evenly around the floor space so that no one area is the main focus of attention.

In the more personal and private rooms of this house in Bali (*top* and *below right*) there is still the same obvious need to filter light by means of shutters. Arrangement of furniture, though, is more intense, more European, than in the public rooms, and highly personal ornaments and decorative elements add to the impression of intimacy.

Simple yet ingenious, naïve yet
sophisticated, these inside/outside
spaces in Kenya (*these pages*) use
local and immediately available
materials to create spaces in which
all normal domestic requirements
are met, though still retaining clear
evidence of their origin in the land
surrounding them.

An open place for people to gather and socialize is essential to the success of public places like hotels, clubs and bars. Both these rooms (*above* and *opposite*), in hotels in Jaipur and Udaipur respectively, former palaces, have exactly the right combinations of low-level seating and filtered light to induce pleasant, subdued social contact while, at the same time, successfully assimilating more exuberant elements into their decoration.

Overleaf

Elegance and refinement characterize this extended and tranquil space
in a Manila house, providing a
marvellous sanctuary in the midst of
the vigorous vegetation that
surrounds it. Enormous low day-
beds dominate the floor-space,
adding to the feeling of peace and
relaxation.

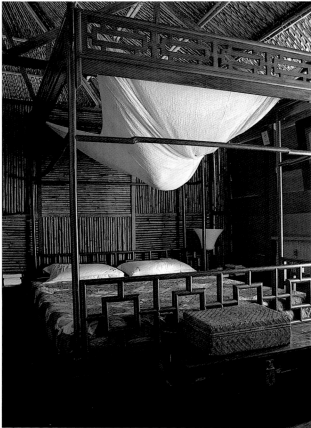

Although there is still a basic simplicity underlying these Oriental interiors, there are distinct notes of high ornament. From an interior decorator's point of view, it is instructive to contemplate how some of these elaborate pieces would translate to, let us say, an all-white minimalist interior of the kind illustrated in the early pages of this chapter. Here, however, they are entirely at one with the decor: a house in Manila (*top far left* and *left*); a museum-house in Bangkok (*below far left* and *left*).

More personal, in a way more ordinary, are the artefacts in these interiors: a garden seat, planters' chairs, a carved chest, figurines. Although the room settings here are drawn from various parts of the East, they still have a common feeling, a constant tension between the utmost simplicity of construction and very complex forms of decoration: houses in Bangkok and Manila (*top right* and *far right*) and, finally, a house in Bali (*below right* and *far right*).

Not surprisingly, the influence of Iberian Baroque is very apparent in the great houses of Manila. Yet in this setting in a nineteenth-century house, the Casa Manila, now preserved as a museum (*left* and *opposite*), the overall effect is really quite uncluttered, mainly because the highly wrought and ornate furniture is allowed sufficient space in which to make its effect.

Overleaf
On the walls of the dining-room of the Casa Manila hang the kind of family portraits associated with the interiors of the European aristocracy or merchant classes.

One of the great houses of Manila, the Casa Manila, is now a museum devoted to evoking life during the Spanish colonial era. Every room has been carefully restored to its period style, expressed in furniture, chandeliers, lamps, paintings, ceramics and general bric-à-brac. The ceilings are painted (*top left*) and often have additional ornament in the shape of elaborately carved wooden friezes (*below left*).

One of the unifying elements in the decor of the Casa Manila is the presence in every room of polished hardwood floors, which beautifully set off the ornate furniture. All the bedrooms have been fully restored (*top right* and *far right*), but the true glories of the place are in the public rooms, where the Spanish colonial furniture, derived from French models, sits beneath ceiling ornament in traditional Filipino styles (*below right* and *far right*).

The combination of an overall simplicity punctuated by ornate and complex detailing in the form of screens, arches and friezes, which characterizes much Oriental design, is especially effective in the layout of rooms for public encounter and conversation. In a private residence, the sitting-room fulfills this function; in public places, like bars and hotels, seating areas must make discreet conversation possible for guests and members – as does this supremely elegant lounge (*above*) in the Temple Club, Shanghai.

Elaborately carved and exotically shaped furniture always looks more pleasing in a very simple context. These two wonderfully organic-looking examples were found, respectively, in Shanghai (*above left*) and Havana (*above right*).

A deep sense of calm after the vicissitudes of war seems to pervade this coolly elegant sitting-room in a large, French-owned private house in a suburb of Saigon (*above*). The orderly arrangement of substantial items of furniture, even the poses of the figures on the wall-hangings, all bespeak a world where quiet and tranquillity are now at a premium.

Even though international tourism has invaded Bali, any visitor will still be able to attest to the skill in woodcarving of the island's craftsmen. Hardly surprising, then, that the grander houses there should have chosen this aspect of local art to embellish their interiors; note the intricate carving of the doors and chairs in this *salon* (*above*). The pictures hang at an angle to avoid reflecting the strong daylight.

Throughout the capitals of Latin America can be found the influence of Iberian Baroque. This dining-room in the Military Circle club in Buenos Aires (*left*) could easily have been copied exactly from an example in a Spanish royal palace.

Modest, yet exploiting every possible decorative opportunity in colour and in the arrangement of a few locally made artefacts, this small dining-room in a house in Zihuatanejo, Mexico, still manages to look inviting (*right*). How effective and dominant in the whole scheme of things is the vase of flowers in the centre of the table – a dramatic note against the green of the dresser.

The success of the arrangement of the *piano nobile* of this house-turned-museum in Manila, the Casa Manila, depends pretty well entirely on the magnificent proportions of the furniture and wall embellishments. A massive table dominates the room from the centre and looks all the more imposing for standing on the bare polished boards of the floor, exactly beneath a fine crystal chandelier. Between the windows two immense wall mirrors hugely increase the sense of space and light in a room where the overall tones are sombre.

IN GRACIOUS AND GRAND STYLES

Places of food preparation and consumption, especially when this is done communally, are of especial importance to the well-being of any house or apartment. There are few more pleasing domestic sights than that of a well-laid table, whatever the extent or complexity of the meal to come. In this Buenos Aires dining-room (*left*), fine white table linen provides the perfect foil to family silver, glass and tableware.

A similar use of furnishing
elements, a similar feeling of careful
and stylish preparation, attends tea
in this Paris apartment (*right*). It is
this sense of self-conscious
stylishness in the way we live and
conduct domestic matters that
forms the subject-matter of the
pages to come.

A sense of family life, still strong in Mediterranean Europe, pervades this table setting in a Sicilian household (*above*). The ritual of eating together is one of the great bonding ties in the life of families; here, taking care over details is clearly considered worthwhile.

Details of preparation for dinner seem to be on the mind of the person assuring the cleanliness of the glasses in this private house in Mauritius (*above*). Through open French windows those who will be seated at the table can also enjoy the close proximity of the long veranda.

The impulse to decorate and embellish our immediate living quarters does not always demand the purchase of additional furniture or ornament. This apartment on the banks of the Nile in Cairo (*above*) has many interesting pieces and features, including a fetching mural on the fireplace wall of the main sitting-room.

Much of the charm of this same apartment is derived from the arrangement of highly personal memorabilia and photographs in carefully ordered display devoted to one of Egypt's most famous singers, Farid el-Atrach (*top left* and *right*). Another Cairo apartment, however, relies heavily for its charm on traditional Arab furnishing and decoration (*above left* and *right*). The seating is made up largely of low-level carved chairs, while open-work screens and window decorations conceal more than they reveal. A frieze of Arabic script completes the upper part of the wall decoration.

The burgeoning economic and social importance of the middle-classes throughout the latter years of the nineteenth century was accompanied by a taste for opulence and ostentatious comfort in decoration, wonderfully exemplified in the interiors of the Castello Falconara in Sicily. Individual lamps and candelabra (*above left*) are so highly decorated that it is easy to forget that their original function was to illuminate. Button-back sofas and armchairs (*above right*) are unashamedly the expression of a society at ease with itself.

Wallpapers are heavily patterned; curtains and other hangings are thick and voluminous; furniture promotes ease at the expense of line; and other features are covered in complex detailing. Even the wooden articles of furniture are elaborately carved versions of a mixture of past styles (*above*).

In one sense, the 'bourgeois' interior was only a more popular re-interpretation of a vision of gracious living that had been traditionally the preserve of the European aristocracy and wealthy merchant families. Nowhere was the vision so elaborately expressed as in the building and decoration of the great houses of the Italian cities of Venice, Rome and Florence. In Venice, whether standing on the Grand Canal or facing on to some secluded square, the city's *palazzi* have always had the finest craftsmanship lavished upon them – in this instance, stuccowork of the mid eighteenth century (*these pages*).

Overleaf
Family portraits gaze upon a scene of faded opulence in the billiard room of the summer palace of the Chigi family, Ariccia, Rome.

The Palazzo Biscari in Catania, Sicily, in 1787 received a visit from Johann Wolfgang von Goethe; although fascinated by the number of antiquities in its apartments, it is doubtful whether the classicism of Germany's foremost writer would have permitted him to enjoy the building itself. The palace (*top left*) is, effectively, a Rococo gem, from the design of the public rooms to the detailing of the furniture. Another curious example of high decoration in the Italian manner is the Farmacia Santa Maria Novella in Florence (*below left*).

The centrepiece of the Biscari palace is the magnificent Salone da Ballo (*this page*), finished in 1772, complete with a frescoed vaulted ceiling around a cupola, fireplaces in the corner niches, and console tables and mirrors. One especial treasure is the exquisite staircase which leads to the orchestra gallery (*top far right*), embellished with more frescoes and stuccowork showing the influence of *rocaille* design, a mainstay of French Rococo.

Built to impress and amaze, filled with antique sculptures, exotic birds, slaves and Moors, the Villa Medici in Rome was the inspiration of Cardinal Giovanni Ricci of Montepulciano. On his death in 1574 it passed into the hands of Cardinal Ferdinando de'Medici, fifth son of Grand Duke Cosimo I of Tuscany. The improvement of the villa and its gardens then became the responsibility of Bartolomeo Ammanati, official architect to the Medici. But, most interestingly, beyond the grandiose effects of the main rooms and gardens lie quiet corners of elegance and interest – small, instructive vignettes (*left* and *opposite*).

There is almost a behind-the-scenes look about these two room settings in the Villa Medici (*above left* and *right*), as though a family may suddenly take up residence within them. It is such settings, and not necessarily those in great public rooms, which can prove most inspirational for more modern decorative schemes.

Simple, yet with an underlying note of opulence, are these two settings, one in Umbria (*above left*) and one in a house on the island of Madeira (*above right*). Note especially how relatively plain spaces can immediately acquire a distinctive feeling of luxury by the use of richly coloured paint schemes.

In the bedroom, a taste for gracious living can be satisfied by close attention to detail – arrangements and objects, perhaps very personal, which are pleasing and distinctive and give importance to an environment in which we spend more time than we realize.

One notable feature of all these bedrooms in Sicilian houses and apartments (apart from one in the Palazzo Chigi, Ariccia, *top right*) is the ornateness of the beds themselves, often the dominant decorative element in the room.

Decoration and the conferring of engaging qualities on any room, especially a bathroom, does not have to be complicated or structural. A simple shower assembly, coupled with a few pieces of elegant furniture, make this bathroom in a Mauritian house (*above*) a place to be enjoyed at leisure.

The fittings themselves are such powerful features in this bathroom (*above*) that very little else is needed to complete its decoration. Once the villa of the princely Odescalchi family and eventually one of the residences of John-Paul Getty, La Posta Vecchia, on the Tyrrhenian Sea at Ladispoli, is now a luxury hotel, but still retains much of the decor of its chequered past, including this bathroom of relatively recent date.

Certainly not grand in scale but entirely pleasing are these two bathrooms which make extensive use of decorative qualities of simple materials. A Chilean bathroom (*above left*) is entirely covered with a kind of crazy paving. In a Marrakesh house a modern Moorish bathroom (*above right*) is enlivened by the use of rose-coloured brick to outline the shower and windows and to form a central floor panel. An antique hanging lamp and terracotta pots provide other decoration.

Both these bathrooms – one Italian (*above left*) and one American (*above right*) – have fittings of the utmost simplicity in retro styles.

In both cases, however, a powerful decorative element is provided by the colour, patterns and form of the floor tiles.

These two Sicilian kitchens (*above left* and *right*) have all the air of welcome that kitchens should have; crockery, ornaments and bottles provide an array of interesting shapes. Kitchen tables provide important surfaces, either for food preparation or as additional eating areas, a function for which the traditional refectory table is ideal.

In an age where the 'dream kitchen' inevitably means something pre-designed and carefully fitted in every aspect, there is something refreshing about cooking and eating areas that seem to have grown up piecemeal, using individual elements of varying age and style, as in this Florida house (*above left*). The presence of wood is always sympathetic to the eye and, here combined with traditional terracotta tiles, looks doubly appealing in this Tuscan farmhouse (*above right*).

The decorative properties of collections of books, objects or paintings are powerful indeed, especially if displayed together. Serried rows of family portraits cover the wall of one room (*opposite* and *below right*) – a kind of cabinet of curiosities – in the summer palace of the Chigi family in Rome, a medieval original transformed into a seventeenth-century Baroque gem (used by Luchino Visconti for the filming of *The Leopard* in 1963). Although much less cluttered, the library of a Swedish manor house (*top right*), now preserved in a folk-museum, makes a powerful decorative effect with undertones of accumulated knowledge and culture.

Books certainly furnish a room and few more splendidly than in the library of the Chigi summer palace; a sense of calm and learning pervades a space already replete with material comforts. The rooms of this palace are decorated in a variety of styles and filled with furniture of all periods – the accretions of time and custom that come with the occupancy of a single family for several centuries. Variously decorated with wall coverings of Cordovan leather, naturalist frescoes, birds both painted and as hanging mobiles, and *trompe-l'œil* paintings, they seem curiously frozen in time. At no point, however does luxury spill over into vulgarity; everywhere there is the happiest kind of opulence and good taste. Similar qualities are abundantly evident in another example of Italian interior decoration in the grand manner – a house in Umbria (*top right*).

At the heart of every thinking-person's house should lie a well-stocked library or book-room, a repository of the intellectual adventures of the owners. These are rooms where the arrangement of the books on shelves imposes its own kind of decorative order, sometimes immaculate, as in this Austrian reading-room in Salzburg (*top left*), sometimes more lived-in, as in this very much used study in a Paris apartment (*below left*). This latter room is also full of objects and furniture that reflect the eclectic tastes of the owners. The actual shelves were made simply from rough planks.

This library-study in a distinguished old Provençal house (*top right*) still retains its original eighteenth-century panelling. The contents of the room, however, are engagingly eclectic and of all periods; the arrangement of the books seems almost deliberately casual. Furniture includes a 1940s cane armchair and, in the foreground, a split chaise-longue of the type known as a 'duchesse'.

In this Paris apartment (*below right*) the library is contained effectively within the *salon* in carefully ordered, enclosed bookcases: a reader's library and music-room, perhaps, rather than a study.

This book-room was created by simply lining the two long walls of the room with shelves. Its pleasant atmosphere of friendly vitality springs from the fact that it is both a workspace and an additional sitting-room, full of unlikely objects. The two plaster caryatids, for example, were inherited from an architect great-uncle of the owner; they were the original models for the decoration of an Art Nouveau building façade. A generally homely atmosphere is further enhanced by the rough tiles that form the floor.

The remarkable interiors illustrated here are the result of meetings of northern and southern European styles at various levels. Drawing inspiration from Italian Baroque palaces in the seventeenth century, then later receiving the attentions of eighteenth-century decorators inspired by French *trompe-l'œil* motifs, the owners of Louhisaari, near Turku, Finland, brought a very special blend of interior decoration to this Palladian villa, originally built in the style known

as 'Baltic Renaissance'. The furniture is a bewildering mixture: Baroque, Rococo, Empire, Biedermeier, and mainly the work of local Finnish craftsmen working from pattern books. Yet everything seems to have its place beneath the beautifully frescoed interior walls. The house is also notable for having been the childhood home of Carl Gustaf Mannerheim, leader of the Finnish people during their struggle for independence from Russia, and their President in 1944.

Although both the decoration and furniture of Louhisaari are eclecticism run riot, there still remains an underlying sense of Scandinavian and Baltic good taste; there is a restraint in the use of the more exuberant elements taken from design cultures further south. This may be partly due to the use of lighter, pastel colours – greys, pale yellows or blues. Within this context there seems no incongruity between a *trompe-l'œil* panel in mid-eighteenth-century French style and a classically proportioned long-case clock of Swedish design.

The influence of northern European
furniture and interior design began
to make itself felt in the Baltic
countries and in Scandinavia during
the late seventeenth century,
reaching a peak in the eighteenth
century. Trade with the German
states, the Netherlands and,
especially, England in timber
produced a return flow of goods
made in wood, so that local
designers became familiar with the
taste in furniture of those countries.
Most of the pieces visible here,
including a fine long-case clock,
were probably copied from English
models, but there is again a
lightness about this arrangement, as
a delicate pale blue picks up the rays
of northern light.

In decorating an interior and arranging objects within it, it is often the transitional spaces – corridors, landings, mezzanines – which present the greatest problems. One solution is to turn them, effectively, into miniature galleries, where collections of objects can be displayed. In the Castello Falconara in Sicily, a long gallery (*above left* and *right*) has become a place of interest and pleasure, with fine furniture and wall arrangements. Above, a line of ornamental hanging lamps lends another, practical focus of interest to the space.

Virtually bereft of all other forms of decoration, apart from fanlights and a tiled floor, this hall in a Burgundy house (*above*) is the ideal setting for a dramatic arrangement of deer heads and antlers. So dramatic is the impact of their pointed, branched forms, that the inclusion here of any further wall decoration or furniture would have seemed superfluous.

This Swedish bedchamber of the Gustavian period (*above*), recreated in the folk-museum of Skansen, Stockholm, may also have been used as a sitting-room, since the bed is arranged along the wall and embellished with drapes swept back from the crowning tester. The chair looks like a copy of a traditional English carver, with a checked linen loose cover in traditional style. A child's chair, bureau and a cot complete the furniture. In the eighteenth century the walls would have been covered in canvas painted to create a panel effect.

If any lesson in interior design is to be learnt from these simple eighteenth-century bedrooms, now preserved in folk-museums, it must be how to create a feeling of comfort with simple means. Hanging curtains from a central tester give the bed space a warm and inviting quality, especially in contrast to the cold surround of bare floorboards. The Swedish example (*above left*) would probably have been considered a fairly extravagant piece in a culture traditionally given to restraint in all matters of style. Restraint is certainly present in this bedroom (*above right*), preserved in the model village of Sturbridge, Massachusetts, a reconstituted rural community, reflecting New England life between 1790 and 1840.

A coolly reticent northern classicism sets the tone of this Swedish dining-room (*above*), now preserved as a museum exhibit; the panelled walls, relieved by large portrait ovals, are painted a characteristic light grey, with highlights in gold. The table, attractively set for a forthcoming Christmas repast, heralded by the sprinkling of flowerets over the floor, is surrounded by chairs which look like simple reinterpretations of mid-eighteenth-century English styles. A classical bust by the window and a chandelier with multiple crystal drops provide two decorative additions to the overall sobriety.

Still focused around an imposing table, but in strict contrast to the retiring quality of the nordic dining-room (*opposite*), is this Tuscan arrangement (*above*) whose lineage might be safely described as Southern Baroque. The curves and complications of ornate cornices and wall mouldings are repeated in the heavy frames of mirrors and paintings – the chairs around the banqueting table, however, reveal an English influence in their simple lines. The enormous Oriental jars make effective but easily removable ornaments. Just visible in the huge mirror on the chimney-breast is the vaulted and decorated ceiling.

The effect is one of direct honesty, sturdiness of construction and suitability for purpose in this traditional Swedish kitchen, preserved in the manor of Tureholm. And, yet, an urge to decorate has been clearly present in the subtle application of the deeper blue to panels, ceiling and door, then extended to the free-standing cabinet. Simple chairs form a contrast to the elaborate wall sconce, while casually arranged blue-and-white crockery makes a pleasing display.

There are few sights more impressive in a domestic context than the shelves of a traditional dresser fully stacked with blue-and-white plates (*left*), an indicator of family wealth. More formal than the display illustrated on the preceding pages, this arrangement in a room in the manor of Tureholm, Sweden, nevertheless retains the restrained homely quality that characterizes so much Scandinavian design. Presumably the presence of the folding table and the simple, decorated dining chairs indicates that this room was also used as a dining-room.

The late Georgian period saw the highest achievements in Irish architecture and design. This wall display of a dinner service above the neo-classical lines of a late-eighteenth-century sideboard with pedestal cupboards (*opposite*) amply conveys the sense of refinement and order of those times. The elegant tapering legs of the furniture suggest that this piece may have been made after designs published in the pattern books of George Hepplewhite and Thomas Sheraton.

Strongly patterned tiling, black-and-white check especially, makes a wonderful space filler in rooms with a utilitarian purpose. The pattern of the floor visually dominates this saddle-room in a Scottish country house (*top left*). A more restrained version provides a decorative backdrop to the brilliantly polished copper pans in this magnificently preserved big-house kitchen in Wales (*below left*).

The careful preservation of this traditional kitchen in a large Scottish house (*right*) does make a point of some relevance to the owners and decorators of more contemporary examples: that the forms, materials and usefulness of the utensils of the past often make them stunning additions to the kitchen, contrasting with modern equipment. The drawback of some of them, like copper saucepans, is that they require a lot of time-consuming maintenance. But others, illustrated here, have the warmth and patina of long-established use: a mortar and pestle, earthenware bowls, wooden trays, a set of scales with weights, and a huge wall clock.

FRANCE

WALES

MASSACHUSETTS

MASSACHUSETTS

SCOTLAND

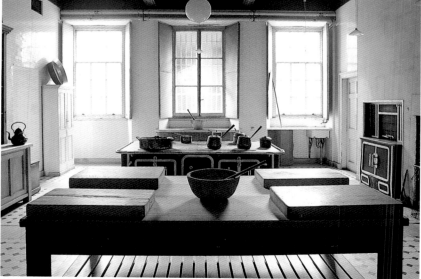

SCOTLAND

The kitchens illustrated on these pages (*right* and *opposite*) are, in one sense, museum pieces, in that they are all in houses that have been restored to illustrate and commemorate the life of bygone times. In another sense, they are immediately contemporary, in that they contain features which are constantly being applied to present-day, working kitchens. All of them emphasize the importance of a good-sized kitchen table, which can be used as an area for food preparation as well as for food consumption. How attractive, too, are the patterns and colours created by dresser-like arrangements of pots and pans on shelves and by large tiled surfaces, especially floors.

MASSACHUSETTS

A sense of spaciousness and light pervades the whole of this fashion designer's holiday home in Saint-Rémy-de-Provence (*above* and *opposite*). What could have been the darkening effect of low ceilings and their supporting beams has been nullified by the overall white colour scheme. Two long kitchen tables, placed together, create a substantial dining surface for family and guests, while the metal chairs can easily be used for other purposes – eating outdoors, for instance. One touch of elegance, though, are the two tall silver candelabra.

In the same house, the kitchen retains the overall white colour scheme of the other rooms, but with subtle additions and variations. The actual units are painted a light shade of grey, while a pleasant splash of colour is introduced in the form of the tiles lining the wall behind the main work units. Bottles, jars and containers in open display provide both practical and ornamental elements.

The beauty of simple things is an ideal well worth bearing in mind in the furnishing of kitchens. Although this Scottish kitchen (*above left* and *right*) has been preserved as a historic example, many of its elements still have immediate relevance today. How impressive is the traditional cupboard, topped by a huge burnished brass dish. The stove, too, has a powerful and welcoming presence and is not so different in form from gas-fired and wood-burning models today.

A kind of grand simplicity marks both traditional Scottish and Scandinavian design – the signature of a specifically northern sensibility, perhaps. Both these arrangements – somewhere between the sphere of the kitchen and that of the dining-room – are in museum settings:

Scotland (*above left*) and Sweden (*above right*). The corner of the room in the folk-museum of Skansen, Stockholm, evokes all the classicism of the Gustavian period, marvellously expressed in the form of a console table with characteristic tapering legs.

As befitting a country subject to long, harsh and very dark winters, a Swedish sitting-room was traditionally dominated by its stove. This example (*above*), in a room preserved in Skansen, is of particularly simple design; often, the stove would have been covered in elaborately patterned faïence, further emphasizing its importance as a comfort to the family and an expression of its prosperity. This room setting is completed by simple rustic furniture, with two sophisticated Neoclassical looking-glasses.

In addition to the warmth from the stove, the traditional Swedish interior was often enlivened by brightly painted furniture: here, in the form of a long-case clock (*above*), which would no doubt have figured among a family's most treasured possessions. In this arrangement of rooms at Skansen, a classic cylindrical Swedish faïence stove is visible through the doorway.

Overleaf
The wall decoration in this traditional Swedish interior may have been intended to imitate marbling, but the use of a quick-dry distemper probably left the painter very little time to achieve subtle effects. The result, however, is one of great graphic boldness and originality, oddly suggestive of massive cell structures.

STYLES FOR COMFORT

The interiors illustrated here and on following pages are a very far cry from the purist minimalism with which we opened this chapter. Their principal aim has been the creation of a warm, protected, comfortable environment, although many of them apply very simple, unsophisticated means to achieve this. In three interiors (*this page*), all in reconstituted Welsh miners' houses, an immediate sense of well-being is induced by the presence of an open fire, a pleasure that can no longer be enjoyed in many contemporary interiors. These fires were also the means for heating food and other items in the small side ovens. Furniture is simple and wooden, but there is plenty of it, including a very fine wheel-back Windsor chair (*top far left*). A third layer of comfort is applied by the plentiful display of what would have been cherished objects: plates, vases, mugs, polished brasses and clocks. The family crockery for special occasions is proudly displayed in a glass-fronted corner cupboard. In a similarly unsophisticated traditional Canadian interior (*below left*) it is a stove that provides that focal point of warmth and energy around which the family would have gathered.

This simple colonial-era dwelling is preserved as a folk-museum near Quebec. The substantial timbers used in its construction and the simple wooden cupboards suggest indeed a land where timber is plentiful and the winters cold. In spite of the massive presence of the elaborately decorated stove, there is an overall severity about the place, a reminder perhaps that Canada, too, has strong connections with that northern aesthetic so forcefully expressed in Scottish and Scandinavian interiors.

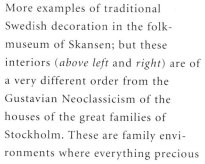

More examples of traditional Swedish decoration in the folk-museum of Skansen; but these interiors (*above left* and *right*) are of a very different order from the Gustavian Neoclassicism of the houses of the great families of Stockholm. These are family environments where everything precious is on display, from the few plates on the racks of the dresser to treasured articles of painted furniture. The table and chairs are rough and rustic, but in a corner stands an elaborately decorated cupboard, the most important piece on view, often a wedding present or the receptacle for the bride's trousseau.

One striking aspect about the wooden furniture in this Canadian interior (*above left*) is how graceful it is in all its simplicity. The chairs, table and double-bodied cupboard have an extraordinary refinement that comes from simple lines and a fitness for purpose. A much more self-conscious attempt to introduce strong decorative elements into a simple interior has been made in this Swedish dining-room (*above right*). There are several examples here of rustic painted furniture, with by far the most elaborate decoration being applied to the most precious objects: the long-case clock and the corner cupboard.

There is a sympathetic quality to wood and to its use in the kitchen in preference to metal, plastic or ceramic surfaces. Here, a wooden dresser and shelving (*above left*) provides an entirely appropriate background to a collection of country pottery in this house in Haute-Savoie, France. Even in a strictly urban environment, the warm tones of a distinctively coloured hardwood can be an agreeable relief from the sense of being surrounded by stone, brick and concrete. This small Parisian kitchen (*above right*) is a veritable haven of delights, all framed in the glow of the surrounding wood, in a modern interpretation of traditional rustic elements.

Wood in the bedroom provides a sympathetic background to the soft furniture usually present. In this house in Haute-Savoie (*above left*), the chalet-like construction gives a pleasantly protected and enclosed feeling to the room, setting off the obvious items of comfort – bed and wing armchair. More spartan in feeling is this traditional Canadian bedroom, although the four-poster and the portraits on the wall suggest that this room was highly regarded within the household (*above right*).

Now preserved in a folk-museum, the interior of the Quebec trapper's cabin nevertheless expresses the fundamental human need for comfort, protection and warmth that its constructors would have felt in the midst of the Canadian winter. A sturdy stove occupies the central position among the simple furniture, while tiny windows are intended to minimize heat loss. The rest of the furniture is of rustic simplicity, and yet its very ordinariness lends it a kind of dignity and modernity.

These two Scandinavian interiors, very different in their degrees of finish, are both in a way expressive of the same traditions. A painter's studio, reconstructed at Skansen (*top left*), is filled with the artefacts of a culture that has a high regard for the materials it uses in design and production: simple yet peculiarly sophisticated wooden furniture and objects, flat-weave hangings and rugs, all within a construction in the material most immediately to hand.

A similar sense of respect for materials is evident in the house (*below left*) designed by Eliel Saarinen at Hvittsträsk, Finland, during the first decade of the twentieth century. There is an integrated quality about the relationship of the furniture and decorative elements of this sitting-room, reflecting the architect's own interpretation of the Arts and Crafts ideal of the family house as a total work of art.

Wood in the house, especially in the form of exposed beams, seems to draw out pleasurable feelings for most people. Is it a sense of being in contact with the structural fundamentals of the building that protects us? In the attic floors of old houses, especially, there is the sense of living with what, literally, keeps the roof over our heads. There is also a secretive, hideaway quality about the cavity just below the roof, wonderfully expressed in these two bedrooms in French houses, one near Grenoble (*top right*) and the other in the central *département* of Allier (*below right*).

These four interiors (*this page* and *opposite*) show how a sense of comfort is built up within a small space by the intense concentration of pattern, texture, small objects and articles of furniture. In this Normandy interior (*above left*), rendered warm and comfortable by the wooden panelling, even a hanging hat and coat take on ornamental value. The decoration of a trailer home presents exceptional problems of space. Yet this home to a family of Parisian performance artists (*above right*) manages to produce effects of comfort and opulence. Everything has been planned so that the majority of the space can be given over to extending the illusion that this is a conventional sitting-room, with rugs, chairs, tables, and chests of drawers.

In the same trailer, the bedroom (*above left*) is a veritable nest of knick-knacks, of soft furnishings and even toys. It is separated from the living space by a heavy velvet curtain that can be drawn back during the day to create extra seating. In some ways, the heavy ornamental effects within the trailer recall the Victorians' taste for intensely patterned schemes in their interiors. This classic example of a nineteenth-century room (*above right*) reflects the standard European styles which were exported to Canada during that period, with a profusion of interlocking motifs on curtains and carpets, here preserved in an old Quebec house.

The effect of books lining a room is welcoming and pleasant in all these interiors (*this page* and *opposite*), yet the overall impression is of book-rooms less finished than those previously illustrated in this book. In the Chiapas region of Mexico, at San Cristobal de Las Casas, lies an institute devoted to safeguarding the interests of the local population. Originally founded in the 1940s, the institute was established in an old seminary and now welcomes volunteers to its pleasantly relaxed rooms; this sitting-room is made remarkable by a fireplace faced in local brick (*above*).

This study (*below left*) is yet another example of the Swedish restraint in interior decoration we have already noted in the many rooms conserved at Skansen. This example, though, makes much more of small ornament and wall display, yet all with a touching humility; as though the user of the desk and books here must have been a worthy but not a grand member of society.

From this photograph (*opposite*) it is easy to see how the arrangement of highly personal objects, furniture and the apparently casual lining-up of the books on the shelves makes this book-room in a Paris fashion stylist's apartment such a success as a comfortable working place.

If ever any recognized style of interior decoration suggested comfort, then it is the English Style. It invokes thoughts of massive, maybe slightly worn, armchairs and sofas, club fenders, and a general atmosphere of *usé* opulence. In fact, this interior (*top left*) – however much it may suggest these characteristics – is part of a converted north London warehouse in which the owners both live and carry on their antique furniture business. A nineteenth-century lamp casts a sympathetic light through a silk shade on to two massive armchairs, a pile of books on architecture distributed between the floor and a nineteenth-century console table; beneath lies a litter of plaster dogs. This space – a study – is separated from a kitchen by Neoclassical columns.

A similar feeling of comfort coupled with tradition is exhaled by this book-lined study in an old Quebec house (*below left*). Again, there is a sense that time is standing still somewhere in the late Victorian or Edwardian era. And how dark wood contributes to this effect!

Although far removed from England, this well-furnished study in a Chilean house has the same well-cared-for feeling that characterizes the other interiors illustrated on these pages. The furniture, however, is conspicuously ornate, while the addition of a guitar hints at the decor's Iberian origins.

Very English is the study at Charleston, the farmhouse in Sussex made famous by the occupancy of prominent members of the Bloomsbury circle. The painting around the fireplace and the design of the fabric of the armchairs are the work of the Omega Workshops, founded in 1913 by the art critic Roger Fry and which promoted the work of young Bloomsbury artists like Vanessa Bell and Duncan Grant.

Though lacking the ostentatiously comfortable accoutrements of the English Style – large armchairs and sofas – this room in a Paris apartment (*above*) manages to convey a very sympathetic, lived-in feeling. The articles of furniture are spare and elegant, but the accumulations of paintings, drawings, books and a well-filled pinboard make for a very agreeable study-type bedroom. There is also an air about the arrangement of objects and furniture that suggests everything came together in an unplanned, accidental fashion.

Comfort, Mitteleuropa style, does have a certain formality about it: chairs, based on eighteenth-century French models, arranged in a formal conversation grouping around a small table; the very deliberate distribution and arrangement of pictures and other objects; the polished wooden floor left bare. Yet, the room is obviously intended as a place where people can meet and converse in a pleasant, welcoming atmosphere, where books and the more treasured collections of the owners of this Budapest apartment can be displayed (*above*).

If the two opposing principles of interior decoration could be described as, first, a search for pure unadorned line and form, and second, a glorying in elaboration and decoration, there can be no doubt where the sympathies of the owner of this Brussels apartment (*these pages*) would lie. Every surface, horizontal and vertical, is filled with additional elements to create a vivid environment in which the world beyond the apartment has little part to play. Dark walls and bookcases create a sense of enclosure, while providing a wonderful counterpoint to the lighter-coloured spines of the books. Everything within the rooms has been called into service as ornament; and in addition to the more orthodox embellishments of paintings, screens, urns and vases, there is a remarkable wall display of the corner sections of antique picture frames.

Dark colours and a flamboyant use of heavily patterned surfaces were two dominant features of the late Victorian interior – or, at least, of its middle-class version (*above left* and *above right*). Heavy woods, notably mahogany, lavish ornament, and Persian carpets would denote the prosperity of a family of standing in town or city. Interestingly, though, there are re-collections in this Quebec house of what the Victorian bourgeoisie no doubt considered to have been the decorative indulgences of the gentry – a trophy head, a library atmosphere, and the ostentatious display of costly objects.

In this Victorian setting (*above left*) the taste of that era for pattern has been heavily indulged: every conceivable surface, including the ceiling, bears a heavy weight of decoration in the causes of comfort and homeliness. Yet, there is a simple Arts and Crafts feel to the furniture, an indication that the latter part of the nineteenth century would engage seriously with issues of design and fitness for purpose. And in contrast to the Victorian decorators, how simply and elegantly this late-eighteenth-century Scottish interior (*above right*) achieves a sense of pleasant warmth; how attractive paintings and furniture look against the green-painted panels.

INDIVIDUAL TOUCHES

Many of the interiors illustrated on the following pages make extensive use of very personal possessions to create highly individual environments. Others derive their uniqueness from a deliberate avoidance of finished decoration. One suspects that the distressed knee-hole desk (*above left*) in this

Paris apartment is rarely used as anything but as a support for other decorative elements in the room. Much more workmanlike, albeit in a very decorative corner against an exposed stud wall, is this finely polished writing table, also in a Paris apartment (*above right*).

Sometimes a working desk can form an interesting focal point within a larger room, a kind of alternative to the main seating area. This can be an especially effective arrangement if the desk or table carries a still-life of unusual objects or small works of art, as in these two very different examples in Paris apartments (*above left* and *above right*).

Accumulation of intrinsically interesting objects is one certain way of building a distinctive atmosphere in any room. This Neapolitan interior (*top left*), for instance, derives much of its charm from the display of examples from the owner's collection of nineteenth-century fabrics, whose rich patterns dominate the decoration of the walls. Other, subsidiary arrangements make this room a veritable cabinet of curiosities: a clutter of books on the table, small pieces of statuary which may once have adorned a cemetery, even dolls' heads among the other *objets trouvés*. A similar sense of casually decorative effects through clutter pervades this Paris apartment (*below left*). Here, the main concentration of disparate objects is on a fine Neoclassical table, in keeping with a general sobriety in the furniture.

The effect of the Paris apartment (*opposite*) that belonged to Coco Chanel might be justly characterized as one of carefully finished opulence. Overall, there is a sense of luxury, but it is not arrived at accidentally. Everything here has its place, from the classical statuary on the mantelpiece to the positioning of the Louis-Quinze chairs; the scale of the objects is as important as their provenance. And everything is still exactly as it was when Coco worked here.

Ease, comfort and privacy: these are the qualities supremely expressed in the form of the traditional wing chair. Usually deeply upholstered, with padded arms, its high back rises to form two protruding rounded 'wings' which protect the occupant's head from draughts or unwanted intrusions. Quite when this form first developed is hard to ascertain, but certainly examples were being made in the late seventeenth century; the basic design retained its popularity through the eighteenth and nineteenth centuries and well into the Edwardian era, when it seems to have acquired its status, along with the Chesterfield, of being the classic seating for clubland. This particular example (*left*), at the farmhouse of Charleston in Sussex, does however retain some feeling of lightness, perhaps because the legs remain exposed and the covering fabric is light in colour. It is much more usual to see distinctly 'heavier' examples, with upholstery, often in thick velvets or leathers, reaching down to short, balled feet. Some interesting attempts have been made in the last hundred years to give a modernist look to the form, notably by Charles Eames in his rosewood and leather 'No. 670' of 1956 and by Arne Jacobsen in his 'Egg' chair of the following year.

In contrast to the relative sobriety of the English example, this Corsican wing chair (*right*) is distinctly flamboyant. All the features of the traditional form – the high back and wings – have been exaggerated to create a fitting piece for an elegant *salon*. Note, too, the cabriole legs, clearly intended to be left exposed.

SEE MORE

WING-BACK CHAIRS   239   249   297   304

Decorative eclecticism is the key principle in the arrangement of this New York apartment. Every room in the house has a different theme, expressed both in the furniture and in the wall decoration. The main bedroom (*top left*) is devoted to the culture of the Navajos; the rugs on the floor, the bed cover and the wall-hanging all have the distinctive strong patterning of their traditional weaving. A frieze around the room represents examples of Navajo pottery. The bed itself is in woven osier. Another bedroom (*below left*) is imbued with the spirit of eighteenth-century Europe, with distinct New World touches, like the rug. The large cushions, bed cover and the armchair are all in twill.

All the bedrooms illustrated here have one purpose – to render any time spent in them as comfortable as possible. Yet, they do have their differences, partly explicable by their locations. In a traditional Parisian apartment (*top right*), the exposed beams of the old structure lend a pleasantly warm note in an urban environment. A bedroom in a Neapolitan house (*top far right*) is yet another display area for the owner's eclectic tastes. A small votive shrine stands on a tripod in the corner; the wall decoration includes an angel's head in *papier mâché* fixed in an abstract metal structure. This Swedish bedroom (*below right*) is the epitome of Scandinavian Neoclassical restraint; note the palette of pale blues and yellows. In a Provençal house (*below far right*) the head and foot boards of the beds pick up the traditional colours and patterns of the region – those warm yellows and floral designs so often reproduced on the textiles and crockery of southern France.

There is an entirely seductive quality about the informality of these two sitting-rooms in a house in the Lot region of south-west France (*top left* and *below left*). They are warm, welcoming and clearly very lived-in. Each of them recognizes the primacy of the fireplace as a main point of focus, around which the collections of the owners' paintings and objects can be arranged. Both of them rely on colour to set the mood of the place – vibrant rugs and furniture coverings and a faded but nevertheless warm background.

SEE MORE

FIREPLACES   234   255   338   340

The fireplaces in these two interiors play a formal role in the overall planning of the rooms. Objects and paintings are arranged around them in an orderly fashion, though with different effects in mind. The exposed brick and distressed wood in a New York house (*top right*) give the whole room a 'country' air, reinforced by the rustic furniture and the 'naïve' paintings on the walls. Again, in a holiday home on the Île de Ré (*below right*), the arrangement of books, paintings and nautical models around the fireplace is carefully ordered, turning the whole wall into an area devoted to the owner's personal interests.

Strong, earthy colours are the very stuff of Provence, to be found in textiles, crockery and, here, on the walls of a traditional house (*opposite* and *right*). Yellow, in warm tones, is especially associated with the pottery of the region; how appropriate, then, that the simple kitchen of the house should be painted in that colour. The ochrous red of the dining-room is also very much a local colour, used both inside and outside houses; it makes a marvellous background for a Cézanne-like still-life on the table. The paints used on the walls have an intensity that is quite unexpected.

Accumulations of objects, personal possessions, clutter, can be turned to good decorative use, making a virtue of creative mess. In a house just outside Paris (*above left*), the owner – a painter and stylist – has marshalled personal effects to create an atmosphere of light and charm. A work-bench and drawing equipment sit happily with old and new furniture, hanging garments and paintings. Other kinds of object make their presence felt by their unusualness in a domestic setting, like these tree sculptures in a Belgian fashion studio (*above right*).

Another Belgian interior (*above left*), part of an apartment right in the centre of Brussels, is much enlivened by the apparently random clutter which fills it. Books lie untidily, while a sense of the surreal is imparted by dummies for clothes display. More orderly is this dining area in a sculptor's studio in Stockholm (*above right*), but again the display of apparently unrelated objects and works of art makes for a space full of interest.

Private rooms – bedrooms and studies – often encapsulate the personal histories of their owners. It is there that we may keep the artefacts and records of the past in the form of possessions no longer used, forgotten toys and playthings. A pleasantly intimate air, for instance, pervades this bedroom in a Paris flat (*above*), as though the occupant had just vacated it.

Decorative licence, the freedom to juxtapose unlikely objects of a personal nature, seems so much more appropriate in a study than in a principal reception room. This private hideaway in a Santiago house (*above*) is full of references to the equestrian interests of the owner.

INHERITED TEXTURES

Homestyle, northern Pennsylvania: this minimally restored interior of a cottage (*right*) near the Delaware river is the weekend retreat of a New York couple, a dress designer and a conceptual artist. The cottage forms part of a larger estate of farm buildings that the present owners use very much in the original spirit of the place. There has been no major restoration, no attempt to prettify – just the effort to carry on life on the farm as it had been lived there for a hundred years before.

What goes around comes around; what was consigned to the rubbish skip twenty years ago is this year's retro style. One notable aspect of this form of interior decorators' nostalgia is a preference for artefacts of the pre-plastics age and a fascination with the modest and the ordinary of the past. In the Tenement Museum on New York's Lower East Side, several apartments have now been reconstituted to reflect life in a tenement between the mid nineteenth century and the pre-World War II period (*opposite* and *below right*). These are the conditions in which the urban immigrants who flocked to the city during that period would have struggled to find some dignity in life. The other kitchens illustrated here – in London (*top right*), in Tuscany (*top far right*) and in Paris (*below far right*) – all make extensive use of fixtures and utensils recycled from a bygone age. What was simple and basic has become chic.

A similar kind of nostalgia to that which makes us value our old pots and pans seems to haunt those owners of old houses who believe that a distressed look is, in some manner, more authentic than carefully finished decoration. The general effect, as in this Belgian house (*above*), is one of constant becoming, of an arrangement of these elements that might finally come together to form the completed environment. The lack of finish does, indeed, allow the display of variegated wall textures and colours; irregular, unsmoothed surfaces are a perfectly legitimate setting for articles of furniture.

The Dominican nuns who founded the beautiful convent of Santa Catalina in Oaxaca, Mexico, almost certainly had no thoughts of deliberately achieving a distressed look in its rooms (*above*). No doubt the interiors owe their simple rough walls to the lack of ostentation appropriate to the nuns' calling. Now transformed into a hotel, the convent offers rooms full of elaborately carved Iberian-style furniture that looks quite magnificent against the roughness of those walls.

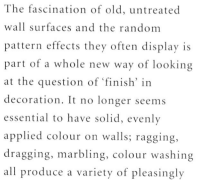

The fascination of old, untreated wall surfaces and the random pattern effects they often display is part of a whole new way of looking at the question of 'finish' in decoration. It no longer seems essential to have solid, evenly applied colour on walls; ragging, dragging, marbling, colour washing all produce a variety of pleasingly irregular effects. The ravages of time, though, cannot be easily reproduced, and the owners of both these interiors – in France (*above left*) and in Belgium (*above right*) – have achieved a dramatic and pleasing effect by simply leaving things alone and letting the echoes of the past tell their own story.

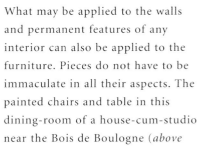

What may be applied to the walls and permanent features of any interior can also be applied to the furniture. Pieces do not have to be immaculate in all their aspects. The painted chairs and table in this dining-room of a house-cum-studio near the Bois de Boulogne (*above left*) wear their visible age with dignity and would lose much of their charm if stripped or given a fresh coat of paint. And rough rustic wood (*above right*), here in a Paris kitchen, does not necessarily need the attentions of varnish or wax.

The principle of minimum intervention has been applied throughout this remarkably beautiful house in south-west France (*these pages*). All the exposed surfaces – walls, floors, ceilings – have been left in the state they were probably in at the end of the nineteenth century. Surprisingly, perhaps, the elaborate forms of period furniture take on an additional allure against the sombre colours of untreated plaster and boards. Fixed features, too, like the fireplaces, stand out unexpectedly.

This graceful seventeenth-century house in Provence is furnished throughout in a supremely eclectic fashion; whatever pleases the owners is included in a brilliant and imaginative way. The bedrooms (*above*) are no exception; this one is made notable by the presence of the oddly shaped *baldaquin* and an array of vigorously patterned flat-weave rugs. In keeping with the untouched quality of the rest of a house in south-west France (*pp. 280-281*), this bedroom (*opposite*) relies entirely on furniture for any decorative effects, created mainly by the voluminous drapes attached to the central tester of one of the beds.

No furniture of contemporary manufacture has even been allowed through the doors of this rough-stone house in Connemara, Ireland. The building itself exhales the savage, mysterious quality of this part of the Irish coast, the very edge of Europe. In all the rooms the basic fabric of construction is exposed; and against the rugged walls and floor is arranged the furniture, all of which unashamedly displays the wear and tear of time and its origins as architectural salvage. Even the doors have been taken from other buildings, like the cast-iron fireplace in the dining-room (*top left*) and the features and furniture of the bathroom (*below left*). The cabinet above the bath was the upper part of a Victorian fireplace, but its cupboards and mirror now make it an ideal bathroom accoutrement. An assortment of furniture of all ages, including a Lloyd Loom table, completes a room of surprises.

The dining-room of a house in south-west France (*pp. 280-281, 283*) continues the theme of other rooms there: arrangements of decorative furniture in a setting of unrestored simplicity (*top right*). Here, though, there is an added feature of interest: the original stone floor. The accidental, random quality of untreated walls is spectacularly evident in this Paris apartment (*below right*), mainly because all the other features in the room have a certain formality in appearance and arrangement, making the wall surface all the more striking. The placing of the large mirror above the fireplace is a strictly classical juxta-position. And the very shapes of the Louis-Seize *fauteuils* bespeak formal elegance, which contrasts with the folding table.

The patina of the past is everywhere in the rooms of this seventeenth-century Provençal house (*p. 205*), originally home to several generations of lawyers. Its latest owner, a Parisian florist, has very clearly decided to let the unique charms of the place reveal themselves gradually, avoiding any over-hasty, comprehensive restoration that could easily destroy the spirit of the place. On the ground floor lies the *grand salon* (*right*) which, at some point in the past, has been stripped of the panelling and mirrors which would certainly have lined its walls. The accidental result is an amazing space in which colour, texture and light combine to create an entirely individual dining-room during the summer months. In winter, the proximity to the garden makes the room an ideal makeshift orangery for the potted plants that need protection from the cold.

Russet reds are everywhere in Roussillon, Provence: every wall, inside and outside, made of locally quarried stone, is tinted by the powder from the amazing ochre cliffs on which the village stands. Even its name is derived from the ochre; the Romans called the place Viscus Russulus ('red hill'). In this dining-room (*top left*) in one of the village houses the presence of the ochre is only too evident. There is also an array of other traditional Provençal colours – yellows and blues – in the form of the pots on the side table.

What is it about warmer climates that makes rough, untreated surfaces so much more pleasant than those where cold, wet conditions prevail? Something, perhaps, to do with keeping interiors simple in the knowledge that much of one's living can be done outside. Simplicity is certainly the keynote of this Mallorcan farmhouse, well inland and far from the tourist crowds of the island's coast. The bathroom (*below left* and *opposite*) is illuminated by small windows let into the thick walls and made of slightly opaque glass that filters the strong sunlight.

In this Provençal kitchen (*top left*), the symmetrical sets of shelves are framed in willow branches cut during country excursions. The materials of the units, too, have a humble origin; they are in fact made of simple rough planks of wood, nailed together. The attractive utensils, crockery and bottles were all found at bric-à-brac stalls in local markets.

Much more obviously finished are these elegant kitchen cabinets in a Paris apartment (*below left*), permitting an almost museum-like display of the owner's crockery. Kitchens, too, can extend the decorative possibilities of any home.

Although the jugs, utensils, baskets in this composition have very different shapes and purposes, the owner of this French kitchen (*right*) has imposed a carefully worked-out symmetry on the whole storage space. On the top shelf, decorative pottery provides pattern in interesting shapes, but even the more practical features, such as the basket and scales, are displayed as though they too were part of an overall design.

Vestiges of the former decoration of this Provençal house remain in the tidily arranged kitchen (*above left*) in the form of wall mouldings and the old cupboards. The whole space makes a pleasant breakfast area and supplementary dining-room.

In more rustic style, the kitchen of a farmhouse in the Cévennes is similarly equipped for communal eating (*above right*). All the pots and pans clearly have their designated place – essential in a kitchen that is also to be used for dining.

Order on a grand scale pervades the restored kitchens of two magnificent houses – one the château of Cormatin in Burgundy (*above left*) and the other the summer *palazzo* of the Chigi family near Rome (*above right*). All the original implements in the Burgundian kitchen are present and intact, including firedogs and the chimney hooks for hanging cooking pots and kettles, known as *crémaillères*. Such displays provide invaluable inspiration for the owners and decorators of more modest properties.

A NEW ECLECTICISM

Clarity in all forms seem to have been the guiding principle for the decoration of this New York apartment (*above*). The soft white of the walls and ceilings and the wood used for the floor maximize the daylight flooding into the room. There are relatively few articles of furniture in a large space and what is there forms a very balanced arrangement. Overall, a kind of modern classicism, emphasized by the pillars, sets the tone. But the classicism is far from strict: the pillars are non-structural and the paintings remain unframed.

Many of the objects in this house near the extraordinary village of Les Baux-de-Provence (*above*) have diverse and exotic origins, yet they have all been marshalled here to form a harmonious and perfectly balanced whole. A magnificent African shield above the fireplace acts as a point of focus. The proportions of the room, too, are such that a normally intrusive element like a staircase is easily accommodated and even forms a stylish additional feature in itself.

Nothing could be more straightforward than the positioning of the furniture in an artist's Paris apartment – central table and ostentatiously comfortable armchairs and sofa around the walls, and large classical looking-glass above the fireplace. Yet there are other levels here that render the place much more interesting: a personal statement in the painting and numbering of certain pieces. Note, too, that the furniture itself has interestingly distressed surfaces.

All the traditional qualities of French interior decoration are on display in a Parisian sitting-room: beautifully proportioned Louis-Quinze furniture in a relatively simple setting. But clearly there are some gestures towards comfort in the form of the strange wing sofa and a 'duchesse' day-bed. Any feeling of formality is dissipated by the presence of loose covers, wooden kitchen stools and other seemingly incongruous objects.

Although this magnificently proportioned sitting-room is in a house in the Cévennes (*above*), there is certainly nothing rustic in the careful balancing of individual elements within it. The defining note is struck by the formal Neoclassical elegance of the Louis-Seize *bergères* ranged in such a way that all attention is directed towards the imposing fireplace. Classical urns and a pair of plaster medallions complete the impression of sophisticated moderation.

In the same way that a successful still-life is created by the pleasing juxtaposition of apparently disparate things, so this Brussels interior (*above*) succeeds in the very deliberate arrangement of varied articles of furniture and decorative objects. The whole room, in an apartment belonging to a film designer, looks like a complete surrealist composition, in which apparent differences are reconciled: a rustic table with vase and formal chairs of various periods.

Leaving the structural elements of a house or apartment still visible within the interior often creates bold decorative effects by contrasting natural textures with smoothly finished surfaces. Exposing the venerable beams in this Paris apartment (*top left*) also achieves an effective counterbalance to the formality of the furniture arrangement, with its focus on the imposing round table.

In shape, the round table is a versatile article of furniture. Sitting around it induces feelings of con-viviality, of being part of a group – in this New York dining space, for instance (*below left*). It can also easily stand alone as a central point in transitional spaces, such as the hall in this private Paris house (*opposite*). In such positions, lit from above, it also serves as a very useful surface for the display of smaller decorative elements.

Both of these interiors show a similar measured and thoughtful approach to decoration on the part of their owners, although in very different contexts. In both cases, though, a monochromatic colour scheme acts as a unifying element. A light, airy sitting-room in a house in Saint-Rémy-de-Provence (*top left*) makes its effect through a relatively small number of pieces of furniture carefully arranged around a low table. There is more detailing in the combination of objects and furniture in this Paris *salon* (*below left*), but a similar sense of order prevails. Most of the sculptures, paintings, engravings and articles of furniture are small, apart from a work-table in wood and wrought-iron. The sofa is in fact a well-disguised folding metal camp bed. Two long mirrors with lead frames mounted on the wall give an extra illusion of spaciousness.

Proper measure in all things clearly guided the fashion-designer owner of this Paris apartment (*top right* and *below right*). Nothing is too much and nothing is too little. There is a sense of comfort, admittedly, yet this is counterbalanced by the undoubted elegance of the interiors, derived from fine traditional furniture and a balanced number of other objects. The whole ensemble feels light and airy, due to the large windows and the looking-glass above the fireplace. The effect of hard uncovered floors is softened by the folds of fabric which, like the walls, are of neutral tones.

Overleaf

There is an eclectic spirit at work in this *salon* in the château of Outrelaise in Normandy, yet the overall effect is one of careful composition. The furniture is a mix of styles – hybrid Louis-Quinze and Louis-Seize, Second Empire in the manner of Louis-Treize, with characteristic turned legs and back, nineteenth-century ease in the form of two capacious wing armchairs and small occasional articles of various dates. The floor is strewn with large Anatolian kilims. Yet, because of the presence of so many unlikely companions, the room has an entirely composed modern feeling, underscored by the choice of colour for the wall panelling, whose vertical and horizontal lines effectively define the space.

The magnificent proportions of this first-floor apartment in a seventeenth-century house in Versailles (*above*) are revealed and enhanced by the careful choice of furniture and the reticence of the decoration. Almost monochrome, the background colour allows the forms of the furniture to assume their true importance. Mixed with the lovingly assembled collection of fine pieces – the owner is an interior decorator of international repute – are objects of rougher texture. For instance, the wood for fuel is prominently arranged as much for its look as its function in a niche that housed a faïence stove.

Cool, pale colours set the tone for a dining-room in a Corsican house (*above*). No jarring element intrudes upon this scene of peace and quiet; even the angles of the high-backed dining chairs are subdued by loose linen covers, discreetly bordered in yellow. All the more dramatic in effect, then, is the interior designer owner's collection of mounted entomological specimens.

BRUSSELS

PARIS

PARIS

PARIS

PARIS

PARIS

The desire to achieve carefully composed interiors, illustrated on the preceding pages, can of course be applied to the less obviously public parts of any house or apartment. Corners of bedrooms, distribution of kitchen units, small transitional spaces (*opposite*) can all demand the attention of the ordering impulse, especially when large numbers of small objects are on display. These may not always be of intrinsic value or even have immediately recognizable decorative qualities. Yet, this corner of the kitchen in a Cévennes farmhouse (*right*) does make a pleasing composition, albeit of Neapolitan coffee-makers, assorted saucepans and two gas cylinders! All these arrangements appear the more powerfully decorative for being positioned against unifying colour schemes.

It isn't always the presence of furniture and artefacts in the same, formal styles that give an interior space a feeling of cohesion. There is considerable variety in the contents of this Belgium painter's studio: covered sofas, Lloyd Loom chairs, books, paintings, busts (*top left*). Yet, somehow, perhaps partly because of the generous proportions of the loft-like space, there is no sense of chaos or even of clutter.

Again, in this New York loft (*below left*) diverse artefacts – painting, Rococo mirror, rustic chair, dining chairs and tables – almost form a complete installation in themselves in the centre of a huge former industrial space.

The owner of this Milan apartment (*top right*) obviously wanted something dramatically visual as a main focal point when she chose an ornamental *pomme de pin*, a much loved object in the decoration of the Louis-Seize period, to stand in such a prominent position in this attic room. Beyond it lies another point of focus, further defining the main axis of the arrangement here: a handsome fireplace surmounted by a grouping of lighted candles. The colour of the walls and the greyish-blue Moroccan tiles cast a soft light over the whole room.

Even in kitchen areas, overall care in how the various elements – fixed units and movable furniture – relate to each other is well worth taking. In this Parisian interior (*below right*), how attractive the table looks as a place to sit, work or eat, placed at a distance from the more workaday installation of cooker and sink. The complexity of the rest of the room – pipes, columns and internal walls – is subdued by the overall white colour scheme.

Beauty and the beast in the bedroom of a Cévennes farmhouse (*opposite*); a decidedly gentle and feminine bed faces a brutal-looking stove across a wide expanse of tiled floor. The balancing effect of the two strong vertical forms is peculiarly satisfying.

As our major urban centres have become increasingly crowded and cramped, so too space and light have acquired a rarity value in the contemporary domestic environment. The pursuit of both is the stuff of completely new lifestyle choices for many people. One solution is to search out larger properties originally intended for entirely different uses – industrial premises, for example – and to convert them to personalized space. One New York couple found this abandoned brick factory in woods in New Jersey (*top right* and *below right*), where their conversion has taken full advantage of the original features of the building – huge windows, rough brick walls – to create a flexible environment for an idiosyncratic mix of furniture.

NEW YORK

NEW YORK

We have already noted how effective attention to detailed arrangement can be in the rooms of traditional living quarters, whether applied to an overall plan or to the creation of 'vignettes' in odd corners or in transitional spaces. In these examples (*this page*), it is the opportunities presented by conversion that have exercised the talents of owners and decorators; basically, these are exercises in how to make areas of comfort and welcome in buildings never intended to engender such qualities: a conversation corner here, a reading area there, and skilful placing of chairs and sofas.

NEW YORK

ARGENTEUIL

The further one strays from accepted conventions in furniture, the more domestic interiors tend to take on the appearance and presence of complete installations. As a centrepiece for this anthology of hard surfaces, the owner of one loft apartment in a converted railway engine shed in Argenteuil has chosen a former dentist's chair, used here as a rest for a small television set. This environment goes well beyond what used to be described as Hi-Tech, in that it deliberately poses questions about the function of furniture and our own preconceptions about comfort in the home.

Continuing the examination of the effect of careful arrangement of various areas of any interior, these compositions in a number of the converted Argenteuil lofts (*this page*), now homes for a group of artists, further demonstrate how the satisfactory effects of detailing can be observed in every part of house or apartment. A low table stands perfectly aligned with the main window of a sitting-room; the pots and pans arranged above the work surfaces of a kitchen seem to be in exactly the right place; a work-station and studio make a compositional virtue out of practical equipment.

In another part of the apartment in Argenteuil (*p. 315*) the sense of a very deliberate installation still prevails, although the overall effect of hardness is mitigated by the simple form of an African chair, underscoring the boundary-crossing nature of the whole assembly – industrial, domestic and ethnic.

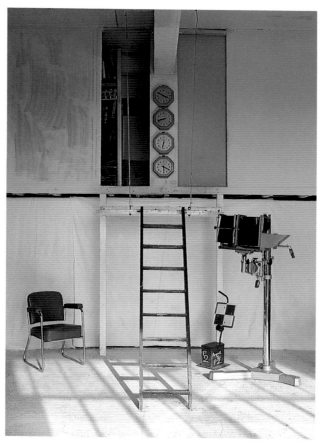

THE WAY WE LIVE | CHAPTER FOUR

AN EYE FOR DETAIL

The finishing touches

TRANSITIONAL SPACES

FEATURES OF FOCUS

TEXTURE, PATTERN AND COLOUR

ORNAMENT AND DISPLAY

'IT'S ALL IN THE DETAIL' is a maxim that holds more true in interior decoration and design than in most other fields of human activity. The finishing touches truly make the broader picture more convincing. The evidence of the following pages is that those touches are many and may not always be obvious. It would be easy to conclude, for instance, that the effectiveness of a decorative scheme could be extended simply by the addition of chosen objects, pictures and general ornament, arranged to complement furniture and furnishings against an appropriate background of walls, ceiling and floor.

But there are many more factors to consider: the treatment of transitional spaces, for instance, those awkward not-quite-certain places, like halls, landings, staircases, mezzanine floors, even doorways, which demand careful attention from the home-maker, since they are not necessarily susceptible to the grand, ordered decorative gestures appropriate to a *salon*. Certain fixtures also act as points of focus within a room; the fireplace is an obvious case in point, although it may be replaced by the stove or the television in certain cultures. Then there are those deviations from the basic foursquare room – alcoves, niches, arches, portals – which can be emphasized and made special by paint and pattern. Texture and colour can be added to the latter on the list of demands on the home-maker's attentions; wall and ceilings, obviously, but also other decorated surfaces dictate mood and feeling in any interior. Then there are the real details, the personal bits and pieces, collections and possessions, free-standing or displayed in cabinets, which are the final extension of that proud urge to create an environment that is a successful reflection of ourselves and in which we find true comfort. And display does not always end with the four walls of the home: it is equally important on patio, terrace and veranda, and in the garden.

Because of its complexity of form, the staircase presents unique opportunities for decorative dramatization. If it is grand, then it should be treated as such, and hung with items of display – paintings, rugs, tapestries – to complement massive carved banisters and newels. While no one in the contemporary world would expect elaborate effects on the scale of the Rococo splendours of the Palazzo Biscari in Sicily, staircases should be taken seriously and not just considered as a convenient way of moving from one level to another. Many of those illustrated on these pages have been made into design features in themselves by the apt choice of paint, the form of the handrail or even the complete absence of the latter. This is especially important for staircases that descend directly into living-rooms, where they must be accommodated as a dominant item.

As areas for the display of pictures and wall-hangings, the walls of the stairwell often offer surfaces larger than those available in the main reception rooms. This aspect has been put to good use in several of the examples which follow, either by using the extended height of the wall surface to display a particularly large artwork or to accommodate a mass of detail such as formal groups of

PARIS

smaller paintings, trophies or other three-dimensional ornament. Even if the staircase is narrow and enclosed and bereft of natural light, it is still an important component in the home and the application of bright, light hues helps to render it a place we enjoy passing through rather than one of gloom and neglect.

Staircases are one obvious feature of access and movement within the home; but there are other important ways of relating living spaces to each other that cry out for the decorator's attention. Corridors and passages are obvious examples where the visual excitements and decorative motifs of other rooms can be continued or find contrast. Let us not forget those glimpses through open doors of rooms and spaces and make sure that the vignette – an arrangement of furniture or wall decoration – framed

by the doorway is itself pleasing to the eye and yet another source of enjoyment as we move about our home.

As a practical way of heating the home, the open fire has long had its day, although most people would agree that the sight of soaring flames still strikes an atavistic chord of welcome, comfort and safety. Even if the widespread use of central heating has meant the demise of the open fire as a realistic daily source of heating, it still survives as an important decorative feature in many homes. Memories of its former importance make it the virtually automatic focal point towards which any arrangement of chairs and tables can be directed. Its traditional form makes it ideal for the display of ornamental objects: the mantelpiece can accommodate all manner of arrangements and even clutter; the chimney-breast is the obvious place to hang an important picture or large mirror. On either side of the fireplace the recesses created by its projecting form can be utilized easily for further wall display or for the fitting of bookcases and cabinets. Let us remember, too, those other features that break up simple foursquare spaces either by projecting into them or leading from them; those secretive corners and alcoves where quiet, secluded activities may occur outside the main areas of the larger room, or the more modest niches and archways of many contemporary

IRELAND

dwellings: all of them are fitting subjects for individualized applications of pattern and colour and, most important, light.

While walls and ceilings are surfaces where the effects of painting, wallpaper and other forms of decoration will be most obviously noticed, less fixed elements can also be used to achieve dramatic effects through the interplay of colour and fabric and the imaginative display of movable objects. Doors – those focal points of interiors and exteriors alike – may be carved, painted to make them blend into the overall decorative scheme or to contrast with it, or left as natural wood or metal to acquire the patinas of age. Movable objects, by sheer variety, offer an infinity of extensions and elaborations to effects of colour and pattern. Small, brightly coloured objects can illuminate and enliven a monochromatic setting: a bowl of *papier mâché* fruit on the kitchen table; a heavily textured and boldly patterned ethnic wall-hanging; a wall covered with paintings in heavy gilt frames.

And individual items of furniture, especially if they are large and elaborate, can in themselves provide everything that a decor needs in terms of pattern and colour. In Scandinavia, for instance, where the decoration of whole rooms tends to be characterized by reserve and restraint, there is a long tradition of applying bold forms in bright colour to particularly prized articles of furniture. Large cabinets may assert their presence through elaborate carving, and such pieces demand that they be given plenty of space so that the full effects of the variations of surface in old wood can be appreciated.

Collecting and the display of collections is perhaps the ultimate refinement of all the urges and drives towards the creation and embellishment of a pleasing habitat that have formed thus far the subject-matter of this book. These are the finishing touches: cabinets of ceramics; display cases of glass; the still-life of a kitchen cupboard; a votive table-top arrangement; a close, orderly grouping of engravings; metal moulds on a kitchen wall. Such arrangements of objects, so important in rendering any interior distinctive and individual, are the new cabinets of curiosities, those collections in the great houses of gentleman-scholars of the seventeenth and eighteenth centuries, which can still serve as an inspiration for contemporary design. Some of the cabinets of artefacts illustrated here are effectively the descendants of those lovingly arranged assemblies of *naturalia* – coral, shells, minerals, gems, plants – and the trophies of travel and trade – antiquities, clocks, fans, boxes, automata and miniatures – which delighted and amazed men of insatiable curiosity three centuries ago. Although such objects have great effect when displayed as groups – rows of baseball masks on a bedroom wall, for instance – sometimes positioned alone they add the final, decisive detail to a table-top, a window embrasure, a mantelpiece. Sometimes, too, the final, telling point is made by the sheer appropriateness of a practical feature: a door handle, a folded towel.

Floral display is instantly gratifying: colour, form, texture and an overwhelming sense of refreshment and renewal; little surprise, then, that garlands, flower-heads and leaf forms should so often have inspired fabric design and painted wall decoration. In their natural state, even within the ordered confines of the cultivated garden, flowers provide that final burst of joyful exuberance that completes the building and decoration of the place we call home. And beyond this garden of delights lie the doorways and arches that promise a world full of possibilities, of new inspirations and cultural challenges.

NAPLES

NAPLES

SICILY

SICILY

MAURITIUS

SALZBURG

TRANSITIONAL SPACES

Staircases, landings, passages, corridors, mezzanine floors: these are the spaces of transition within the home. In their comparative awkwardness, they can prove a great challenge for the decorator. Staircases, in particular, capture the imagination; if they are wide, sweeping and monumental, then they do present a marvellous opportunity for the grand gesture (*these pages*). This can be in the form of display – of paintings or trophies – or in sculpted and carved newels and banisters.

NAPLES

A staircase, if light and open, can bring a wonderful sense of spaciousness to the very heart of a building. These two very different examples do exactly that. The open-work of the painted handrail of the staircase in the Musée des Beaux-Arts in Saigon allows light to stream down through the stairwell (*left*). In the Rococo Palazzo Biscari in Catania, Sicily, the staircase which leads to the orchestra gallery (*opposite*) has turned the narrow passage that separates the Salone da Ballo from the windows of the façade into a major decorative feature. Its vaulted ceiling is decorated with frescoes by Lo Monaco, while the exquisite stuccowork of the ceiling and of the staircase itself show the influence of French *rocaille* decoration.

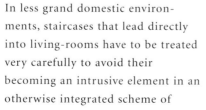

In less grand domestic environments, staircases that lead directly into living-rooms have to be treated very carefully to avoid their becoming an intrusive element in an otherwise integrated scheme of decoration. Both these examples – one in Devon, England (*above left*) and one in Quebec (*above right*) – make their entrances unobtrusively and look very much part of the room itself.

These two staircases have the virtue of turning the spaces they occupy into places of additional design and architectural interest. Both of them are decorative features in their own right. One, in a traditional house in Mallorca (*above left*), brings a sense of sculptural scale to a low-ceilinged room. In a seventeenth-century Provençal house (*above right*), the main staircase adds a note of grandeur to a simple entry hall.

LONDON

BRUSSELS

PROVENCE

ROME

NEW YORK

LONDON

Staircases can influence the whole mood or feeling of a place by their very forms (*these pages*). Straight staircases fit reassuringly into the spaces to which they lead. Curving staircases and ones that disappear from view and then reappear inevitably excite an atmosphere of mystery or even of the sinister. This example, for instance, built as part of a film-set in the Cinecittà studio complex, Rome, looks like some visionary nightmare construction from Piranesi's *Carceri*, or 'Prisons' (*top right*).

ROME

NAPLES

TUSCANY

GRENOBLE

PROVENCE

CHILOÉ

PARIS

NEW YORK

PARIS

IRELAND

PROVENCE

BUDAPEST

NAPLES

BURGUNDY

All the staircases illustrated here
(*opposite*) have been made into
central decorative features in houses
which vary from the modest to the
grand. All of them, however, have
the advantage of being interesting
forms in themselves, twisting and
turning their way from one level to
another. And many of them have
been used by their owners as
additional display areas, of paintings
or three-dimensional objects.

Of an entirely different order is the
staircase that stands foursquare in a
main living-room, like this example
in a Belgian house (*right*). In spite
of its central position, the staircase
is somehow still just part of the
overall scheme of things, benefiting
from the height and extent of the
room.

A supreme example of the use of the stairwell and related landings as areas for display is this modern metal staircase in a converted cheese factory in Milan (*left*). The generous proportions of the whole stairwell, enhanced by open treads and thin steel ribs, make it an ideal place for positioning furniture as an extra surface for the display of ornaments.

Less useful as display galleries are the very simple staircases illustrated here (*opposite*). It should be noted, however, that all of them succeed in looking attractive, mainly because the colours of the walls transform a dark and narrow transitional space into one of light and neatness, yet all of them present a slightly different solution to the simple act of getting upstairs.

CHILE

PROVENCE

SICILY

PARIS

PARIS

LONDON

DEVON

CHILE

GRANADA

PROVENCE

STOCKHOLM

CHILE

333

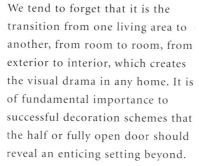

We tend to forget that it is the transition from one living area to another, from room to room, from exterior to interior, which creates the visual drama in any home. It is of fundamental importance to successful decoration schemes that the half or fully open door should reveal an enticing setting beyond.

A deliberately unfinished doorway in a Cévennes farmhouse leads the eye to another interior and a window on the outside world (*above left*). The bold colours of the upholstered furniture in this Paris apartment (*above right*) are clearly picked up and continued in the next room.

Open doors in a Burgundy château (*above left*) reveal a succession of elaborate panel decorations, each forming a visual set-piece when viewed in the frame of the doorway. Seemingly inspired by the colours of *commedia dell'arte* costumes, the passages in this Paris apartment (*above right*) are decorative items in their own right.

Overleaf
Looking to something beyond: in all these examples from around the world, the photographer's eye has picked out the promise of the next space, the next room, in vignettes framed by door-posts and lintels.

IBIZA

ÎLE DE RÉ

PARIS

PROVENCE

PARIS

IRELAND

IRELAND

UMBRIA

UMBRIA

IRELAND

UMBRIA

NAPLES

VERSAILLES

PARIS

PARIS

PARIS

STOCKHOLM

BUENOS AIRES

PARIS

BALI

GOA

PROVENCE

BRUSSELS

ROME

BRUSSELS

WALES

SCOTLAND

FEATURES OF FOCUS

In any interior, there are certain permanent features that merit the decorator's special attention, in colour, material and position. These include doorways and windows and that supreme point of focus, the source of heat. In these examples (*left*), it is towards the fireplace that the whole arrangement of the room has been directed. It is the feature – in both cool and warm climates – which is often the most elaborately worked in terms of shape and additional decoration. Even real estate agents inevitably identify a surviving original fireplace in a property as a major attraction.

IRELAND

MOROCCO

CANADA

PARIS

PARIS

PARIS

The mantelpiece is the obvious display surface for the most precious objects of a household and the chimney-breast the obvious place to hang a work of art or large looking-glass. In a Paris apartment (*top right*) the classic French fireplace exerts a strong individual presence amid the Louis-Quinze furniture, with which it is however entirely in keeping, almost as an additional important piece itself.

Very different is this cottage fireplace in Connemara, Ireland, although it too is clearly the most dominant feature in the simple sitting-room (*below right*). Its bright colours provide the occupants of the house with a very different palette from that of the greys, greens and browns of the surrounding countryside.

PARIS

TUSCANY

All these fireplaces (*left*), through their sober classical shape, impose a sense of order and formality in the rooms where they stand. They are relatively high in terms of overall ceiling height and the eye is constantly led to focus on them by the addition of other elements: a painting, two pots, a large looking-glass and a shrine-like arrangement of objects and pictures.

NEW YORK

PARIS

The light colours of these fireplaces (*right*), in rooms with white or near-white walls, make them initially less of a presence. However, in all these cases, their form and importance has been re-emphasized by the number of objects and wall decorations that surround them. Even the hearth and the spaces created by the side pillars have become areas for decorative display.

ÎLE DE RÉ

ÎLE DE RÉ

PARIS

IRELAND

Part of the importance of the open fireplace – at least when in use – is due to the visible flames. In countries where the closed stove is the traditional form of heating, notably in Scandinavia, the stoves themselves became room features in their own right (*these pages*). They were designed in shapes which reflected the stylistic preoccupations of the time and were usually clad in highly decorative faïence. Their height, too, made them a dominant presence in any room, although it was customary to position them in a corner rather than before a central chimney-breast.

BUDAPEST

STOCKHOLM

STOCKHOLM

STOCKHOLM

STOCKHOLM

STOCKHOLM

MOROCCO

MOROCCO

In an earlier chapter, we saw how important an entry door can be in the overall external architecture of a building – a focal point to be elaborately decorated and embellished. Similarly, internal doorways, niches, arches and alcoves, any original features that add to the charm and complexity of an interior, can themselves become the focus of special decorative effects or arrangements of objects and furniture (*these pages*). Doors can be painted or carved; their surrounds can be decorated in colour or plaster relief; niches and alcoves can be filled with pots, baskets and books; varying levels of wall created by pilasters and arches can be picked out by special painted treatments; and articles of furniture and statuary can be given greater prominence by being placed in a recess or beneath a vaulted part of the ceiling.

VERSAILLES

NEPAL

STOCKHOLM

STOCKHOLM

ROME

AMALFI

MOROCCO

ROME

345

TEXTURE, PATTERN AND COLOUR

The impulse to decorate and elaborate our immediate environment is common to many cultures, and embraces both grand and humble settings. Both these examples of sumptuous wall embellishment are clearly extremely grand, yet there are differences in intention and purpose. The owners of Louhisaari, a 'Baltic Renaissance' house, north of Turku in Finland, were originally inspired by the styles of the great Italian Baroque palaces and decorated their own externally austere mansion with elaborate fabrics and tapestries (*left*). Simple beams were augmented with carvings and then painted, another feature of an interior that certainly does not mirror its exterior.

Italianate, but on home territory, are the great rooms of the summer *palazzo* of the Chigi family at Ariccia. In the larger reception room, great panels of Cordovan leather, embossed and coloured, give the walls a sumptuousness that threatens at times to overwhelm paintings and furniture alike (*opposite*).

Much more than their successors – even more than the practitioners of Rococo – the decorators of the great Renaissance and Baroque houses regarded the interior wall as a surface to be elaborated and embellished by every possible means. Sculptured, painted and gilded, the rooms of the great French châteaux of the early seventeenth century scarcely needed furniture to complete their decorative schemes.

The panelling of such splendid living quarters was generally one of two types: *de hauteur*, which treated the whole wall as a unified decorative surface; and *d'appui*, where the wall was divided into two distinct levels, sometimes by a cornice or by recessing. In one of the great rooms of the château of Cormatin in Burgundy (*top left*) the differentiation between upper and lower parts of the wall is quite startling, but carried off successfully by the sheer magnificence of the painted and gilded decor. Equally elaborate in its own way, and again divided in two, this panelled room in Salzburg makes its effect through ornamental carving and the patina and texture of wood rather than through colour (*below left*).

Built during the first decade of the seventeenth century, later associated with the literary circle of Madame de Sévigné and her cousin Roger de Bussy-Rabutin, the château of Cormatin is one of the gems of the reign of Louis XIII (*top right*). The walls of the great rooms combine meticulously carved wood with paintings of exceptional quality, which include landscapes and architectural subjects. Beams have been left exposed and painted. Non-decorated walls were hung with tapestries. But how strangely superfluous the furniture looks (*below right*)!

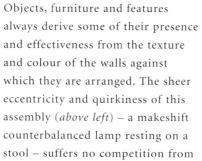

Objects, furniture and features always derive some of their presence and effectiveness from the texture and colour of the walls against which they are arranged. The sheer eccentricity and quirkiness of this assembly (*above left*) – a makeshift counterbalanced lamp resting on a stool – suffers no competition from the rough monochrome of the wall. Lines, wherever applied, usually suggest simplicity and order. Here, their neurotic twitching (*above*) conveys very deliberate decorative intent, especially seen in combination with a heavy gilded frame and 'chair'.

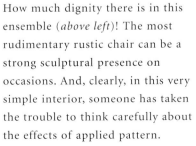

How much dignity there is in this ensemble (*above left*)! The most rudimentary rustic chair can be a strong sculptural presence on occasions. And, clearly, in this very simple interior, someone has taken the trouble to think carefully about the effects of applied pattern.

Wall-hangings are an immediate way of introducing colour, texture and pattern to otherwise monochromatic interiors (*above right*). Rugs, kilims, bag-faces, weavings of various kinds, are effective bringers of history and culture to washed walls.

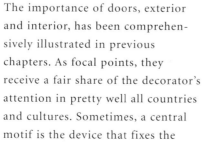

The importance of doors, exterior and interior, has been comprehensively illustrated in previous chapters. As focal points, they receive a fair share of the decorator's attention in pretty well all countries and cultures. Sometimes, a central motif is the device that fixes the door's importance. This ancient Moroccan door in carved wood is dominated by the rose form, above other polychrome panels (*above left*). Similarly, a wrought-iron panel at head-height is the major decorative element in this Art Deco door in Budapest (*above right*).

Touchingly, decoration and the bringing of pleasing effects into the home, affects us all, humble and grand alike. This door, straightforward in construction, now preserved in one of the houses at Skansen, Stockholm, has clearly inspired someone to make a decorative effort – to extend the large-scale marbling effects from the walls and to add a frame where no moulding exists (*above left*). In contrast, the overwhelming presence of a door (*above right*) in the manor house of Plas Newydd, Wales, leaves no doubt about the importance accorded to this particular entrance by the original builders.

Overleaf

In the present age, the ceiling seems to have become neutral territory in decoration. Since Victorian times it has not attracted the attentions of plasterers and painters in any significant way. These examples show just how effective this feature could be.

UMBRIA

UMBRIA

ROME

UMBRIA

KENYA

MOROCCO

MANILA

MEXICO

SICILY

MANILA

ROME

FLORIDA

355

ROME

BURGUNDY

SWEDEN

PROVENCE

KENYA

GUATEMALA

NAPLES

BALI

PARIS

CANADA

BURGUNDY

MANILA

NAPLES

UMBRIA

LUXOR

CAIRO

MOROCCO

COMOROS

MARSEILLES

SUSSEX

COPENHAGEN

SANTIAGO

GUATEMALA

GUATEMALA

357

CANADA

SWEDEN

FINLAND

MALLORCA

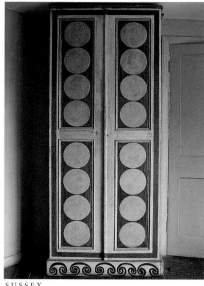

SUSSEX

BANGKOK

MAURITIUS

SWEDEN

SALZBURG

Preceding pages
There are so many ways to harness colour and texture to decorative effect. Attention to the minutiae of interior arrangement is one of them: juxtapositions of small objects, of hangings, of paintings, of furniture, even of foodstuffs, real and imitation. And inspiration for such 'vignetttes' can be found on our travels or in other parts of the home.

What can be applied to the fixtures of the home as colour and pattern also has a clear function in the embellishment of the movable items. Painted and carved free-standing furniture, especially cabinets and cupboards, enjoys a long and honourable tradition in many cultures (*left*). In all cases, such powerful pieces do need careful positioning in terms of background colour and light to achieve their full effect. Sometimes it is more effective to allow the colours and textures to assert their presence through arrangements on the furniture rather than by application to the piece itself, like this beguiling collection of shells in a small Mauritian museum (*opposite*).

MASSACHUSETTS

NEW YORK

FRANCE

KENYA

FRANCE

FRANCE

FRANCE

MANILA

FRANCE

NAPLES

FRANCE

NEW YORK

ORNAMENT AND DISPLAY

The urge to collect may take many forms and be directed in countless ways, but it is undoubtedly a very powerful one. The members of the scholarly European gentry who filled their cabinets of curiosities in the seventeenth century with a diversity of artefacts, or the English aristocrats who assembled their collections of classical antiquities and Renaissance paintings during the Grand Tour, probably had something in common with a more modest, contemporary spirit of acquisition. And with the urge to collect – not always, but usually – goes the urge to display. And with display comes a whole range of engaging decorative effects: glass-fronted cabinets full to overflowing with personal memorabilia or with carefully ordered ceramics; table tops covered with contrasting forms and materials; walls brought to life by paintings, drawings or heavily textured hangings. In their own different ways, all the arrangements illustrated here (*opposite* and *right*) are, effectively, individual 'cabinets of curiosities'.

PARIS

PROVENCE

PARIS

WALES

CHILE

FLORIDA

PARIS

PARIS

PARIS

IBIZA

IBIZA

As a means of creating pleasant environments, display should certainly not be confined to the principal living areas of the home. Kitchens, bedrooms, staircases and landings all have their claim to this aspect of the home-maker's art. Kitchens, because they are usually so full of interesting shapes and intriguing objects, present marvellous opportunities for display, and usually look the better for it when it is done with sensitivity to colour and form (*left*). Crockery – if attractive in shape and design – looks wonderful on open shelves. Other types of utensil, including bowls, wooden trays, implements of the pre-plastics age, can adorn work surfaces or dresser shelves. Humble metal moulds make intriguing wall arrangements.

STOCKHOLM

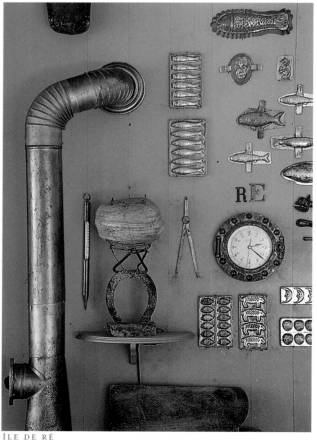

ÎLE DE RÉ

SEE MORE

KITCHEN LIGHTING   109   291   308   311
STOCKHOLM HOUSE   269   444

Around the kitchen, there are always certain specific areas that invite special attention. The dresser, or dresser-like work surfaces and shelves were designed for display, nowadays combining the expected accoutrements of the kitchen with more conventional ornamental elements (*top right* and *top far right*). But even the more obviously utilitarian features, like the kitchen sink, make a much more positive contribution to any overall design if everything around them is ordered for colour and form (*below right* and *below far right*).

MOROCCO

IRELAND

MASSACHUSETTS

FRANCE

BRAZIL

PARIS

IRELAND

BELGIUM

CORSICA

PARIS

PARIS

KENYA

BELGIUM

KENYA

SUMBAWA

PROVENCE

Sometimes it is the telling detail that makes the strongest decorative point in a room. All the objects illustrated here (*opposite*) look intriguing because of their form and inventive wit, yet none of them necessarily impress by being significant works of fine or decorative art. Indeed, many quite humble objects and utensils can make an effective contribution to our visual pleasure through careful placing or juxtaposition. The entirely original wall display in this New York bedroom (*right*) is composed of baseball masks from years gone by – a theme echoed by a bed and table made partly of baseball bats and balls.

Most immediate, most colourful of all decorative displays, of course, are flowers, bringing the colours and scents of the garden to interior and exterior alike (*above left* and *above right*), or inspiring a cornucopia of delights in the form of a mural (*opposite*). Around the home, they can bring vibrancy to any corner of the most uninspiring room; outside, they are the life of our own private enclosures, courtyard or walled garden (*overleaf*), from which doorways lead us to the vibrant life of the streets beyond (*pp. 370-71*).

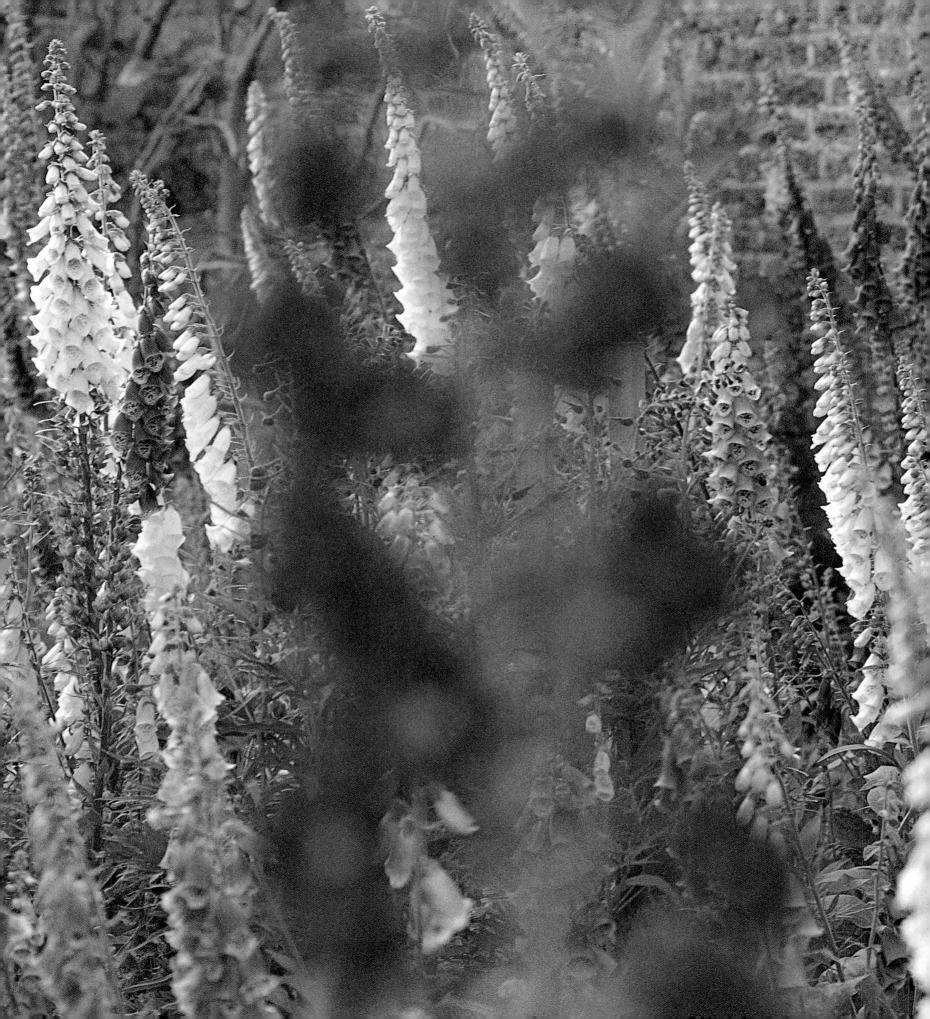

THAILAND

BALI

SHANGHAI

MOROCCO

CUBA

ROCHEFORT

SHANGHAI

ROME

POMPEII

SICILY

CHILE

GOA

JUST LIVING

Outside the home

AROUND THE HOUSE

ON THE STREET

THE MARKET-PLACE

CELEBRATING PEOPLE

THE SEARCH FOR A SATISFACTORY LIFESTYLE, expressed in the arrangements of interiors to assure our warmth and shelter, comfort, and ultimately aesthetic satisfaction, is a powerful driving force. Yet, we also belong to a wider world, local, regional, national, and ultimately international. In the pages of this book we have looked at styles and expressions of taste from around the world; we have seen many differences, but we have also discovered an amazing number of similarities and connections, extending the usefulness of this book as a compendium of possibilities.

Thus, the richness of Oriental furniture may render it stunningly decorative when arranged in an all-white western modernist interior; an African chair has a humanizing effect on a grouping of heavy-duty, metallic 'furniture'. We begin to inhabit this world of multiple choices as soon as we move beyond the confines of our immediate domestic context, first to the extensions of our home, and then to the streets and markets beyond, whose own detailing, vibrancy, colours and shapes are yet more sources of visual inspiration and refreshment.

First, however, we impose ourselves on the areas immediately around the home – extended and open if in a warm and benevolent climate, or confined and closed if, say, a roof terrace in a northern city. In either case, such spaces can be truly an immediate extension of the rooms themselves. Furniture and ornament, too large or unwieldy for indoors, may be effectively disposed there. Even a modest roof terrace can become the 'room outside' with the addition of a couple of formal potted plants, a table and four chairs. The choice of furniture in such spaces, though, does need careful thought and attention; certain pieces, too finished and elaborate, can easily strike an incongruous note. Simpler forms and materials – cane, canvas and unpolished hardwoods – are often more appropriate. These are the places for alfresco dining, conveniently situated close to the kitchen, but also open to garden or even urban skyline. City terraces especially can evoke the entirely satisfactory feeling of being small corners of peace and tranquillity far from the sounds of traffic and the overwhelming presence of towering masonry.

Again, a special boon during warmer months, or in those climates with the good fortune to enjoy year-round fine weather, is the backyard or loosely delineated patio. Less architecturally structured than the formal veranda or terrace, it permits outdoor dining and relaxation simply

MARRAKESH

with the aid of a few chairs and perhaps an ad hoc awning.

Such arrangements are clearly a far cry from the formal courtyard or enclosed garden, although they share the essential quality of being places of transition. In Islamic and, to a large degree, Mediterranean culture in general, the court is an integral part of the domestic structure; by way of the shade cast by arcades the rooms of the interior are seamlessly connected with the fragrant plants of the central open area and, traditionally, with the soothing sound of gently bubbling water. Few of us are fortunate enough to enjoy the use of courtyards on the scale of the Moorish and Hispanic examples illustrated here, but they give us every reason to reflect on how we can make use of confined external spaces for the display of formal planting, large-scale ceramics and even statuary.

Living compound-style seems to strike a chord in all cultures – is there some buried recollection here of groups drawing together in a defensive circle to guarantee their warmth and security? Certainly, Balinese courtyard architecture, a practical expression of lives spent in constant movement between the inside and outside, has proved one of that island's durable cultural exports, influencing design and architectural practices throughout south-east Asia and the Pacific region. Again, open space around the house allows the architectural arrangement of large potted plants and even cultural and religious icons and, evitably, some water feature. Sometimes, however, our decorative ingenuity in relating our homes to the land around need not extend further than the simple setting-down of table and chairs in a pleasant and secluded spot and the preparation of a colourful and enticing spread. Even the impromptu, however, calls for a conscious attention to detail – perhaps in the choice of table cloth or crockery – for the full potential of the situation to be realized.

And so to our engagement with the community at large. Beyond our gardens and patios are the streets and squares, the buildings, which define the architectural and physical character of where we live, unless of course we have decided a rural isolation will be our dominant lifestyle. For most of

CHILE

us, however, as town and city dwellers, the shops, bars and restaurants are the places where we experience the world at large, where we find ourselves as part of the wider human network of styles, relationships, endeavours and cultures. In the Western world, the bar or pub is a universal institution, dispensing solace and camaraderie to the gregarious and to the lonely. In other cultures, the tea-house may serve the same purpose, and indeed the sight of a group of men in explosively animated conversation over glasses of green tea in any Islamic town or city is instantly memorable.

The more formal cousins of the bar, restaurants, are as varied as the cultures to which they belong and as full of inspiration; they are exportable, however – Chinese restaurants in Latvia, Greek restaurants in Melbourne. But in terms of the authentic, vibrant life of the street, there is little to better the experience of eating and conversing in restaurants or cafés that are a direct expression of the surrounding cultural fabric. Nowhere, except in south-east

TUNISIA

Asia, would a hawkers' market or Chinese tea-house seem entirely convincing; and how utterly natural it seems to eat, feet dangling in a river beneath the tables, at a popular open-air restaurant in Manila.

Good restaurants the world over use produce that is immediately and freshly available for the majority of their dishes, which argues a close relationship with that other concentration of human exchange, colours, scents and general vitality – the market. Is there any place more seductive than a group of stalls groaning under piles of fresh and colourful fruit and vegetables, or alive with the blooms of the season, or with the shallow trays of the day's catch? How fastidious are the displays in the best markets, usually arranged by the producers themselves, and how fastidious and conscientious are the buyers in any truly great market – touching, smelling, before finally committing to the all-important purchase. It was Elizabeth David who once remarked that the tourists who spend so

much time in art galleries, museums and cathedrals might also consider the local food markets as part of a city's cultural heritage.

A similar visual excitement to that of the brilliantly colourful market stall is exhaled by the traditional open-fronted shop, especially if the merchandise is of all shapes and sizes and, most important, in abundance. In these days of supermarket and shopping mall, what relief the small shop, still retaining its original façade, offers. In any street such shops, cluttered and crammed with goods, give us the sense of changing pace, of moving in a slower, more considered way. Something of the same quality is attached to the small workshop, especially if the activity is artisanal. We know there is no going back to a William Morris-like vision of a craft utopia, but it is important to value those places where human endeavour and skills still have a direct relationship to the quality of the finished article. These are the splashes of colour as the world becomes more monochrome.

SUMBAWA

At the end of this chapter appear some of the people who inhabit those places illustrated in quite remarkable profusion and variety on the foregoing pages; they go about their business in street or market, eat and drink in their local restaurants and bars. The cycle continues: we return to our homes with ideas and acquisitions, with the colours, life and energy which inspired us. Each in his or her own way continues to contribute to the whole human endeavour: to create satisfactory living spaces in whatever circum-stances and make them one's own.

AROUND THE HOUSE

Somewhere halfway between the private and the public world, verandas, terraces, backyards, patios and, eventually, gardens provide places for eating and drinking, conversation, reflection and contemplation. In warm climates a loggia/veranda may very well serve almost as an additional room or gallery. In the Bragança Palace in Goa (*left*), this gallery provides enough shelter for a significant extension of the collection of furniture and objects in the main rooms within.

Open to the garden but still well sheltered, the loggia of a Guatemalan house (*opposite*) still provides space for furniture; most importantly, there is seating, making it a real area of transition from the interior rooms to the world without.

Overleaf
The uses to which verandas and loggias can be put are many and varied. If wide enough to accommodate tables and chairs, they are clearly ideal extra dining areas; in any case, they are wonderful places for simply sitting. They are useful places, too, for keeping objects whose material and size make them unsuitable for interior display, like large earthenware pots, or outsize baskets, or caged birds. Formal indoor furniture can look out of place here; more successful schemes are achieved with cane, twig or rustic chairs and tables.

MAURITIUS

MAURITIUS

MAURITIUS

SICILY

MAURITIUS

SAIGON

SICILY

BUENOS AIRES

SANTIAGO

NAIROBI

MEXICO

BURUNDI

379

This wide and accommodating loggia (*right*) runs along one side of a magnificent private house in Mauritius. It is clearly wide enough to provide a conversation area behind the woven blinds which unroll to filter the strong sunlight. Part of the house, yet at the same time an extension of the garden, this is a transitional space between two experiences. It also complements the dining-room, just visible at its far end (*p. 177*).

BALI

SAIGON

MAURITIUS

FINLAND

CANADA

MANILA

All the seating areas illustrated here (*opposite* and *overleaf*) show the flexibility that the veranda can have as a place accommodating the activities of the home – eating, drinking and conversation – while introducing the delights of the garden to its interiors. The form of verandas and terraces varies, of course, according to climate and topography. In sunny, sub-tropical regions there is an obvious concern with shade, protection and alleviation of the effects of heat. In alpine conditions, a veranda like one in a chalet near Grenoble (*right*), can take full advantage of whatever light and warmth there is, and offer the fullest possible view of mountains beyond.

MOROCCO

BORA-BORA

CAIRO

BALI

SAIGON

SRI LANKA

PROVENCE

NORMANDY

ÎLE DE RÉ

PROVENCE

TUNISIA

ÎLE DE RÉ

Verandas and terraces are of very
deliberate construction, very
distinctly part of the houses to
which they are attached, though
they usually present an opportunity
to partake of the pleasures of
surrounding garden or plantation.
On the upper floors or roof, though,
they can be entirely secluded. Less
enclosed but equally attractive and
useful is the variously named
backyard or patio, an ambiguous
area sometimes only defined by
paving, walls or perhaps an awning.
These examples (*opposite*) make the
point that a pleasant outside dining
area need not depend on an
elaborate construction; all of them
make use of a space immediately
adjoining the home, but in an
engagingly informal way. In some
cases, it has only been necessary to
introduce chairs and a table to an
area within easy reach of the kitchen
to create an atmosphere of warmth
and conviviality, perhaps
embellished by formally trained
vegetation and some shade from
open sunlight. All of these elements
are brought together in a peculiarly
satisfying way in this brick-paved
area outside a house in Hammamet,
Tunisia (*right*).

Enclosures, courtyards, walled gardens are of a very different order to the verandas and terraces illustrated on preceding pages. For one thing, they do not offer any *aperçus* of the world outside, the surrounding garden or landscape. In effect, they are additional rooms in the home, though open to the sky and even filled with formal vegetation and water features. Grand courtyards, like this one in Naples (*top left*), are ideal spaces for the display of monumental works in stone, often combined with ornamental planting. More modest, more informal, a Paris garden (*below left*) reinforces a feeling of privacy by a profusion of plants and trees around its borders. Such an area, within a heavily built-up city, inevitably assumes a secret, hidden air. The planting is formal, but not oppressively so; and the central area is defined by clipped trees and four large terracotta pots in a traditional Tuscan design.

SEE MORE

FOLDING TABLES   285   334   407

The enclosed garden, with its central axial pool, symbol of paradise, of the house yet not of the house, is one of the most refined expressions of Islamic art and architecture. Porticoes lead from the dwelling to the scented, watered space at its heart, making the transition from indoors to outdoors scarcely noticeable. Planting is usually minimal – box hedges, potted orange and lemon trees, myrtle bushes. Water is all-important, befitting its status as the differentiating element between survival in a civilized environment and the desert. Among the greatest achievements of the Islamic architects of Moorish Spain are the gardens of the Alhambra and the Generalife in Granada (*top right*) and (*below right*). They are also an expression of that quintessential Mediterranean feature, the patio or court, which can be created or imagined whenever there is an enclosed space: a few terracotta pots on a paved area, the sound of a gently bubbling fountain, the shade of vines trained around a pergola or of an olive tree.

Although this Marrakesh house dates, in fact, from the seventeenth century, its central area interprets the time-honoured Islamic court in an entirely contemporary way (*right*), yet with a sufficient number of antique features to underscore its authenticity; all the finely worked doors, for instance, are taken from an older building, as is the sculpted ogival arch that surmounts the entry to the court. The floor tiles pick up the motifs of Berber weaving. And the whole space is additionally defined by four orange trees around a low bubble fountain and – in the evening – four illuminated lanterns of traditional Moroccan design.

The gardens and courtyards of the West use water in a concealed way; even the traditional fountain is based on the sudden energetic appearance of water and then its disappearance for recycling. In Islamic courts (*above left*) and (*above right*) the bubble fountain, often scented with strewn petals, ensures that water is a constant presence, refreshing just by being heard. Both these Marrakesh courts are arranged around the central water feature, then further defined by carefully placed minimal vegetation.

The Moorish courtyard, understandably, became part of the Spanish vernacular in architecture. In this form it was exported to the Spanish colonial empire to grace the great houses of the capitals of Latin America – here, in Havana (*above left*). In an Andalucian courtyard (*above right*), another important feature appears: since the space is open to several storeys, it is usual for it to have one or more galleries, leading to the upper rooms.

Defined by high building, the courtyard provides an especially sympathetic frame for sculpture, both figurative and abstract, and for other large objects whose very size may preclude their proper display in an interior room. Any of the oppressive effects of enclosure can be softened by the judicious placing of vegetation and by arcading. A Rome courtyard (*top left*) is entirely dominated by classical statuary, bringing a strongly formal air to it. But in this gloriously untidy space in a Granada house (*below left*), plants are positioned haphazardly among the varied shapes of terracotta pots and bowls.

The acquisitive eclecticism behind the varied assembly of textiles and objects inside a Neapolitan house has evidently spilled over into this intriguing courtyard (*top right*). Large potted plants, placed on different levels, increase the feeling of mystery around unusual table and wall decorations.

Almost on too grand a scale for its immediate surroundings, this fountain in the courtyard of a Guatemalan house is indeed monumental (*below right*). Everything about its form looks overblown and exaggerated, an impression deepened by the placing of additional potted plants around the rim of the basin.

Size in courtyards really does matter, at least in terms of the effect they produce within the building. Neither of these two examples – one in a public garden in Delhi (*top left*) and the other in Granada (*below left*) – induces quite the same sense of secretive enclosure as those illustrated on the previous pages. Both have an openness derived from their size relative to the enclosing building, giving them a feel half-way between a court and a square. One expects that any significant human activity will not take place in the central area, but in the shade of the surrounding arcades.

The arched and vaulted arcade is one of the most important architectural attributes of the traditional courtyard. It acts as an area of transition from interior to exterior, from shade into light. It also provides scope for additional decorative forms: varieties of arch, sculpted columns and capitals, tiled floors and even wall-painting. In a house in Hammamet, Tunisia, the space and volume of a small courtyard are divided and articulated by a simple arrangement of vaults and arches, enclosing a fountain (*top right*).

Still showing the Moorish influence, but in Westernized fashion, this courtyard in a magnificent Seville house (*below right*) provides space for eating and conversation beneath its formal arches. The central area is given up entirely to a very deliberate arrangement of potted plants around a fountain.

It would be hard to imagine more pleasant environments than these two Islamic courtyards, one grand and spacious, the other secretive and intimate. An imposing arcade – so large that it can easily accommodate rows of potted plants – surrounds a vast courtyard in a Granada house (*top left*). The variety of architectural features creates an ever-changing play of light and shade.

In a Cairo garden (*below left*) the atmosphere is almost impossibly idyllic. Everything in the design vocabulary of the Islamic garden has been brought together to create a unique place of deep peace, yet also of visual excitement. A central fountain surrounded by a ceramic basin in tiles of traditional design provides the main focal point; a recessed alcove has become a kind of day-bed; and the whole is completed by a varied array of potted plants, to make the perfect secret garden.

The same intricacy and detailing that characterizes Islamic filigree-work also informs the long tradition of woodworking in north Africa, notably in Egypt. Beginning with the Fatimid dynasty – responsible for the founding of Cairo in the Middle Ages – a magnificent line of craftsmanship in wood stretches to the present day. This skill and artistry can be seen in doors, panelling, but especially in the kind of open-work so appropriate for the low-level screens which line the galleries around the central well of the traditional domestic courtyard. This example (*top right*) is in a house in Marrakesh.

More subtle, and more finely worked are the screens and friezes defining a Cairo courtyard (*below right*). Texts from the Koran create a fascinating play in elegant Arabic script against the background repeat pattern of the woodwork.

SEE MORE
OPEN-WORK SCREENS   78   155 167 179 447

It is often said of traditional Balinese building that it is an architecture of courtyards. Even modern houses on the island still consist of a series of pavilion-like structures arranged compound fashion around a number of courts. A central area serves as a place for communal living; a court within a court, to the north-east, is the site of the house temple where the gods of the island's unique mixture of Hinduism and animism are celebrated.

A large house in Ubud (*right*) enshrines all the traditional Balinese architectural virtues, yet in an entirely contemporary way, creating independent spacious interiors that nevertheless relate to each other within an overall plan. This flexibility in form has made the Balinese style a much imitated model in vernacular architecture throughout south-east Asia and the Pacific region, and even Australia.

Enjoying life around the house and the joys of eating alfresco does not necessarily demand a specially constructed courtyard or deck. Sometimes it is simply a matter of setting up a table within reasonable proximity to the source of food and in agreeable surroundings. Visual effects are still important; a vibrantly coloured table cloth in a meadow near Bordeaux (*top left*); a seaside spread at Arcachon on the French coast of the Bay of Biscay (*below left*).

All manner of elements can be combined to elaborate and extend the function of the 'outside room'. In a Corsican house belonging to an internationally known interior decorator (*right*), the rooms flow seamlessly into a terrace located next to a 'natural' swimming pool.

The terrace, or formal area for relaxation, can also effectively be located away from the immediate vicinity of the home. Because of the spectacular views available from this particular spot in a Balinese garden (*top left*), the owners decided to create a paved area to accommodate day-beds and a parasol, making a vantage point to look out over the dramatic hill scenery of the island.

In a French garden (*below left*) an impromptu dining area has been set up in a place made wonderfully attractive by trees and borders in combination with old iron gates and well-weathered masonry.

This spot near a Tuscan house does not look at first sight the most obvious place to set out a group of chairs, presumably for social purposes (*top right*). Yet, look closer, and there in the background is the classic Tuscan landscape beloved of poets and painters, of hills whose forms are punctuated by the tall fingers of cypress trees. The white sweeping forms of the chairs, too, offer an invitation to a sculptural gathering beneath the tree.

If one seeks shelter for the outside dining area, then this structural arrangement in the garden of a Mallorcan house (*below right*) would come pretty close to being the perfect solution. Hemmed in on all sides by lush vegetation, the area is sufficiently shaded to make the use of sunshades, awnings or parasols almost superfluous.

Overleaf
The combination of sunlight, terrace and planting, orderly or riotous, is universally irresistible as a setting for alfresco eating.

IBIZA

PROVENCE

ARGENTINA

TUSCANY

BELGIUM

CORSICA

SICILY

MOROCCO

MEXICO

RHODES

SWEDEN

IBIZA

SEVILLE

PROVENCE

PARIS

GUATEMALA

CORSICA

IBIZA

CORSICA

TUSCANY

CORSICA

IBIZA

FLORIDA

CUBA

BOMBAY

BUENOS AIRES

ATHENS

COPENHAGEN

ON THE STREET

Beyond the home, beyond its immediate surrounding features, lie the streets, the main arteries of communication for the community in village, town and city. And along the streets lie the communal meeting-places: bars, restaurants, cafés, shops and markets. These are the places of exchange: goods, money and conversation, clearly an important commodity in most of the bars illustrated here (*opposite*). And without conversation a bar can seem a very doleful place indeed (*right*). By and large, though, these are the places where we seek a certain atmosphere, where we spend time in convivial company, and from whose decor we may even derive some inspiration.

DUBLIN

Bars across the world come in all shapes and sizes, from the cool and cosily intimate to great roaring beer-halls, where the last things on offer are peace and quiet. In general, though, they are content to declare themselves as places of varying degrees of sociability and conviviality, from Sri Lanka (*top left*) to Rome (*below left*). And even though the array of bottles behind this Marrakesh barman's head is sparse indeed (*opposite*), a smile confirms the café as a place of welcome and human warmth.

SAN FRANCISCO

NORWAY

ATHENS

MARSEILLES

PARIS

CAIRO

The difference between eating out in a restaurant of one's choice and eating at home is almost as great as that between theatre and real life. Attendance to the rituals of presentation and protocol bestow a special status on the food thus consumed. Restaurants themselves, of course, come in all shapes and sizes (*opposite*) and vary as much in atmosphere as domestic interiors. There is nothing quite as engaging as the Italian, French or Chinese family restaurant, where dishes have evolved over the years and the interior has remained untouched by the interior decorator. Sadly, we now have to travel further and further afield to find such places, although once there we will be forgiving of any culinary shortcomings.

Among the world's restaurants, the hawkers' markets of south-east Asia (*top right* and *below right*) offer the consumer an amazing array of food. Almost as amazing as the choice are the prodigious feats of memory by which stall-holders recall who has ordered what and from which table.

BALI

BANGKOK

SAIGON

BUDAPEST

Deserted, restaurants demand that we judge them as they are – temples to food that only fulfill their purpose when completed by the clientele they await. In their very different styles of decor (*left*), they are a kind of secular equivalent to those other places of escape from the pressures of urban life: the churches and temples. And how much we need such retreats: a strangely beatific expression in a tea-house in Saigon (*opposite*).

SALVADOR DI BAHIA

SAIGON

Carefully prepared food, attractively
set out on a long table, is alluring in
itself. Rice, crayfish, vegetable,
chicken, with a traditional
Vietnamese sauce, make an irresistible composition on the table of
a French-owned private house in
Saigon (*opposite*). The additional
features required to make the
experience of eating more entertain-
ing are not always immediately
predictable: in this restaurant in
Manila (*left*) the feet of the diners
are refreshed by the river that flows
beneath the tables.

For those who take the preparation of food very seriously indeed, there is an almost religious intensity in the handling and preparation of the raw materials. Like the organized churches of the world, the kitchen is a place of hierarchy and ritual. Also, one hopes, of joy in this very vital activity; certainly that emotion seems evident on the faces of the kitchen staff in a popular Italian restaurant in Mexico City (*above*). The pared-down functionality of professional kitchens can be a style inspiration in itself, as witness the Hi-Tech movement of the 1970s.

Restaurants the world over are often family businesses, small units where everyone has a distinct idea of his or her position in the order of things. In a land of plenty, like Provence, a family restaurant – this one near Les Baux-de-Provence (*above*) – inevitably reflects the produce available at local markets in the dishes it offers. Thus is maintained an intimacy between the processes of cultivation and husbandry and that of consumption.

SALVADOR DI BAHIA

SALVADOR DI BAHIA

THE MARKET-PLACE

The fresh food market is the first step in the distribution of foodstuffs from kitchen garden, from farm and plantation, from field and orchard, from river and sea. Leaving aside the supply chains to supermarket and processed food plant, the market appeals to that deep human wish to acquire raw food in as fresh a condition as possible. And nowhere is this more true than in the fish and seafood stalls the world over (*this page*).

SANTORINI

COCHIN

Most markets impress by their colours and the simplicity of their presentation. In fish markets, especially those on the quayside illuminated by the intense light off the sea, the brilliance of the hues and the boldness of pattern make for delicious visual preliminaries to the pleasures of cooking and consumption. Pinks and reds combine with silvers to gleam and glow with phosphorescence in the fresh rays of a coastal dawn – here, in Tangier (*top right*). And all the colours of the ocean rainbow hang in a quayside fishmonger's in Valparaiso, Chile (*below right*).

MANILA

A market is a place of abundance and of richness of display: colours bright and fresh, whether arranged singly or in pyramids (*top left, below left* and *overleaf*). Thank goodness, what is on sale varies from place to place, country to country, but we recognize the authentic market the world over by its evocation of 'plenty', by the display of tomatoes, peppers, courgettes and aubergines in any Mediterranean town, or by the towering arrangements of guavas, papayas, pineapples and breadfruit in the tropics. The breadfruit – proudly displayed by a Balinese chef (*opposite*) – is native to the Pacific Islands. In 1793 it was introduced to Jamaica by Captain Bligh of *Bounty* fame in the belief that it could become the staple food of the slave population. The scheme was not a great success, but Jamaica does remain a major producer.

COCHIN

SRI LANKA

TUNISIA

BOMBAY

LUXOR

BANGKOK

MEXICO

LUXOR

SRI LANKA

NEPAL

SALVADOR DI BAHIA

BANGKOK

NAPLES

BANGKOK

MARSEILLES

BURUNDI

BANGKOK

MAURITIUS

MAURITIUS

The imagery of the market-stall, whether a boat in Bangkok or a food counter in Burundi, is among the most potent in our appreciation of the good things of life and as close as many people get to the wider natural world. The imagery is rich in colour, texture, form and pattern, brought to life by the presence of people, often producers, in the processes of exchange. This is a world of buyers and sellers meeting with immediacy impossible in more rigidly formal environments (*these pages*). Sometimes the two parties come together in unplanned, spontaneous ways; this roadside market in Burundi developed as an almost impromptu happening (*overleaf*). One man's meagre display is another's cornucopia; but however rich or spare the presentation, there is always the prospect – warm and reassuring – of acquisition and eventual consumption.

BURUNDI

BURUNDI

BALI

PROVENCE

MOROCCO

MAURITIUS

MAURITIUS

ROME

Whether a neighbourhood market in Paris, Rome or London or a village or country-town market in Morocco or Mauritius, the gathering together of people and produce is a real point of focus for a community, and any visitor. It is an opportunity for the exchange of views and gossip; and the feel-good fallout from the presence of so many good things is incalculable (*these pages*). Elizabeth David, surely the greatest English writer on food matters, found a unique joy in the sheer volume and variety on display in a good market: tomatoes, courgettes, peppers, melons, asparagus, strawberries, redcurrants, cherries, apricots, peaches, pears and plums. Her remarks were largely confined to descriptions of the markets of Provence and Italy, but her enthusiasm powerfully evoked the feelings aroused by food markets throughout the world.

GUATEMALA

SALVADOR DI BAHIA

NAPLES

NEPAL

MAURITIUS

SHANGHAI

MOROCCO

If a market convinces by its displays of foodstuffs in abundance, the traditional open-fronted shop makes an initial impression by its stock. There are few sights more depressing than a retail outlet with just a few items for sale. Again, just as in the market, a rich and exciting display is all-important; unusual bric-à-brac and the utensils of the domestic environment, as well as foodstuffs, all tempt us, if their arrangement is sufficiently intriguing: baskets, cooking pots and pans, ewers and storage jars (*these pages*).

Overleaf
To be valued in the age of the shopping mall and supermarket, the small shop front has achieved the status of a folk-art form. Unlike the bland uniformity of the chain stores and retailing giants, here form, colour and individual ownership really count.

CAIRO

IRELAND

MAURITIUS

LUXOR

WALES

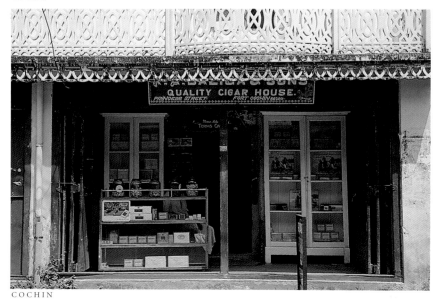

COCHIN

CAIRO

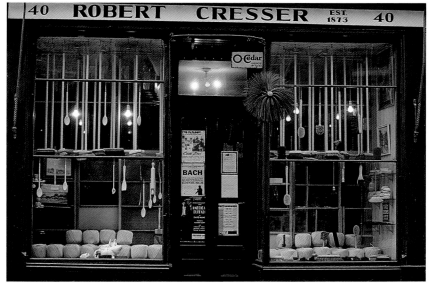

SCOTLAND

IRELAND

DELHI

MANHATTAN

TUNISIA

ATHENS

MEXICO

SHANGHAI

MANHATTAN

CAIRO

BANGKOK

IRELAND

Preceding pages
This general store in Chiloë,
southern Chile, has variety of stock
in profusion. The number of
different items, the cupboards and
shelves, even the counter, crammed
with goods for sale, make for a
peculiarly reassuring impression;
this is a place where shopping would
be a distinct pleasure and which
epitomizes everything we miss about
old-fashioned retailing.

In some of the domestic interiors
illustrated in previous chapters, we
noted that clutter and creative
untidiness could actually produce
living quarters just as pleasing in
general feel as immaculately planned
and furnished spaces. At a time
when retail outlets have become a
focus for fashionable contemporary
design, it is undoubtedly refreshing
to experience a change of pace by
wandering into some emporium
selling no matter what, but where
there is abundance, an absence of
planning, and entirely engaging
disorder (*these pages*).

SAIGON

SEE MORE

CHINESE FURNITURE   167   378

DELHI

MAURITIUS

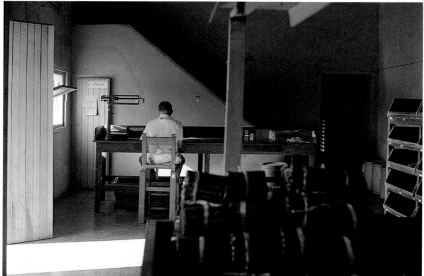

CUBA

MASSACHUSETTS

MARRAKESH

MARSEILLES

CELEBRATING PEOPLE

As an illustration and celebration of the way we all build, design and live, it seems appropriate that this final section of the last chapter should be devoted to people caught in various circumstances – some unaware – around the world. In virtually all cases, the response to the camera is marked by dignity and enjoyment of the human condition. And it is perhaps in a small atelier or workshop, beating pots or rolling cigars, that this enjoyment is most palpable among people at work (*these pages*).

DELHI

BALI

CHILE

ROMANIA

BANGKOK

ROMANIA

GUATEMALA

GUATEMALA

The photographs on these pages evoke the very essence of 'just living', whether in wedding feast preparations in Romania (*top right*) or the re-enactment of nineteenth-century rural life at a reconstituted village farm in New England (*below right*). All these people (*opposite*), wherever they may be, are in the process of defining their lifestyles, of simply living around the home or in that indispensable area – the garden or backyard – which is its immediate context; they are somewhere between doing something and just being there. Yet, in the apparent simplicity of these environments, the number of choices, of preferences expressed in matters of style and design, is quite limitless – colours, materials, textures and, most important, how they all fit around the particular human group.

SALVADOR DI BAHIA

NAIROBI

STOCKHOLM

CHILE

CHILE

ARGENTINA

TUSCANY

SANTIAGO

CHILE

MEXICO

GUATEMALA

SALVADOR DI BAHIA

Nothing quite engages feelings of sympathy for our fellow men as the single moments of vulnerability – sometimes posed, but usually not – caught by the camera. These vignettes are the stuff of life around the world (*opposite*), insights into other worlds, other lives, other pretensions, other preoccupations, but ones with which we can all identify. And if the subject is caught unawares, the effect of a fleeting moment increases tenfold (*right*).

SAIGON

Something of a lost art in television-obsessed Western society: serious conversation in an all-male group in Delhi, a city where vigorous debate is still a cherished activity.

Conversation, especially in public places (even in the shade of a stone elephant) is one of the most pleasant activities of the urban environment – being 'urbane'. All great cultures have been characterized by the quality of public exchange, whether in formal debate or on the café terrace: Athens, Rome, Florence, the London of the coffee-house, the Paris of the *salon*, Hindu and Muslim cities everywhere. And when such meetings are rendered difficult by political pressures or the general deterioration of city life, so the whole culture suffers too.

Overleaf
This section is essentially a celebration of some of the many people who inhabit the villages, towns and cities illustrated in this book. These are the folk, some stopping for the camera, who follow their own traditions and create their own environments according to their needs and means and thus make their own important contribution to the human collective.

SEE MORE
DECORATIVE STONEWORK   357   370   371   387

DELHI

CAIRO

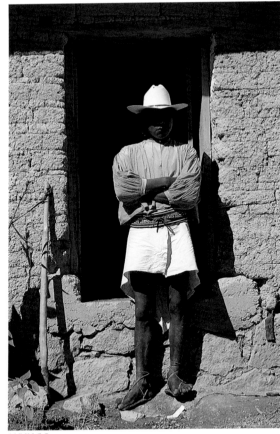

MEXICO

CHILE

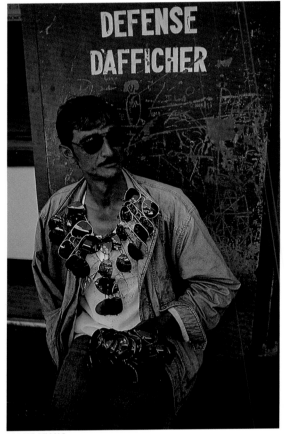

MAURITIUS

GUATEMALA

LUXOR

HAUTE-SAVOIE

ROMANIA

GUATEMALA

CANADA

CANADA

MEXICO

GUATEMALA

MEXICO

SICILY

NEPAL

NORMANDY

NEPAL

BELGIUM

NORMANDY

COMOROS

GUATEMALA

MEXICO

ROMANIA

COMOROS

Before designer labels and peer pressure, children can show as much individuality and joy in their dress as in their surroundings (*opposite*); pleasure is evident on the faces of these Mexican children (*right*) in all the finery and exuberant colours of traditional costumes.

Overleaf
These children create their own enjoyment without any special clothing or equipment in an almost timeless scene on the Brazilian coast at Salvador di Bahia.

Pages 454–55
The diversity of human life and experience throughout the world has been comprehensively illustrated in this book. Yet, touchingly, how similar we can all appear and how strong the bonds of the group, no matter what the size, when we are bound by a sense of community, a culture and a common goal.

ROMANIA

ROMANIA

MAURITIUS

CHILE

CHILE

MEXICO

INDIA

ROMANIA

MEXICO

BURUNDI

KENYA

SCOTLAND

IBIZA

IRELAND

BURUNDI

PARIS

NAPLES

NAIROBI

NORMANDY

JODHPUR

FRANCE

DELHI

FLORIDA

NORMANDY

CUBA

LONDON

MALLORCA

The environments we create (*previous pages* and *left*), the interiors we decorate and personalize, from Ireland to Ibiza, from Naples to Nairobi, from Burundi to Brussels, are there to be lived in and enjoyed. They should serve and satisfy us and, at the same time, stand as a contribution to the greater world we have designed. Contentment with what we have created may be found in many shapes and forms; here (*opposite*) the nomadic hamlet (in Kenya) of an internationally renowned wildlife photographer is open house to family and friends of all species.

BRUSSELS

CUBA

PARIS

PARIS

MALLORCA

MAURITIUS

A final note of pride and celebration in stunning colour: at harvest festival time, every household in the Filipino village of Lucban on the island of Luzon tries to outdo its neighbours in the opulence and brightness of its display of flowers, fruits and produce (*opposite, right* and *overleaf*). In some cases, frames are constructed before the façades to make them larger and more impressive. Whole streets are decorated end to end with columns and garlands of ravishing colours and textures – a truly individual art form. And the prize for the best display is a water buffalo!

THE INDEXES

A guide to
design and style
ideas

DECORATIVE FEATURES
ACCESSORIES, FURNITURE
AND FURNISHINGS
INTERIORS
FABRICS, MATERIALS,
DECORATIVE TECHNIQUES
COLOUR, TEXTURE
AND PATTERN
STYLES AND DESIGN
GENERAL INDEX

ACKNOWLEDGMENTS

Designed by Stafford Cliff
Text and captions Robert Adkinson
Production artwork Ian Hammond
Index compiled by Anna Bennett

All photographs
© 2003 by Gilles de Chabaneix

Design and layout
© 2003 by Stafford Cliff

Text and captions © 2003 by
Thames & Hudson Ltd, London

The Way We Live © 2003 by
Thames & Hudson Ltd, London

Published by
Clarkson Potter/Publishers
New York, New York
Member of the
Crown Publishing Group,
a division of Random House Inc.
www.randomhouse.com

Clarkson N. Potter is a trademark
and Potter and colophon are
registered trademarks of
Random House, Inc.

Originally published in Great Britain
by Thames & Hudson Ltd, London
in 2003

Printed and bound in Singapore

Library of Congress Cataloging-in-
Publication Data is available upon
request from the publisher.

ISBN 1-4000-5134-7

10 9 8 7 6 5 4 3 2 1

First American Edition

Dedicated to
François de Chabaneix, Françoise Winter, Catherine, Martin & Simon de Chabaneix

Very special thanks are due to the many people who have contributed to the realization of this book,
especially to Stafford Cliff who had the original idea. I also wish to thank Catherine Ardouin, Jean-Pascal
Billaud, Catherine de Chabaneix, Daniel Rozensztroch & Francine Vormèse, who accompanied me on many
of my travels, and Martine Albertin, Béatrice Amagat, Françoise Ayxandri, Anna Bini, Marion Bayle, Marie-
Claire Blanckaert, Barbara Bourgois, Marie-France Boyer, Marianne Chedid, Alexandra D'Arnoux, Jean
Demachy, Emmanuel de Toma, Geneviève Dortignac, Jérôme Dumoulin, Marie-Claude Dumoulin, Lydia
Fiasoli, Jean-Noel Forestier, Marie Kalt, Françoise Labro, Anne Lefèvre, Hélène Lafforgue, Catherine
Laroche, Nathalie Leffol, Blandine Leroy, Chris O'Byrne, Christine Puech, José Postic, Nello Renault,
Elisabeth Selse, Caroline Tiné, Claude Vuillermet, Suzanne Walker and Rosaria Zucconi, who helped me to
discover the world, and Mattias Bouazis, who helped me to classify all my photographs.

The following people and organizations were generous in allowing me access to their houses and
apartments: Jérôme Abel Seguin, Jean-Marie Amat, Avril, Peter Beard, Bébèche, Luisa Becaria, Dominique
Bernard, Dorothée Boissier, Carole Bracq, Susie and Mark Buell, Michel Camus, Laurence Clark, Anita
Coppet and Jean-Jacques Driewir, Bertile Cornet, Jane Cumberbatch, Geneviève Cuvelier, Ricardo Dalasi,
Anne and Pierre Damour, Catherine Dénoual, Dominique and Pierre Bénard Dépalle, Ann Dong, Patrice
Doppelt, Philippe Duboy, Christian Duc, Jan Duclos Maïm, Bernard Dufour, Flemish Primitives, Michèle
Fouks, Pierre Fuger, Massimiliano Fuksas, Teresa Fung and Teresa Roviras, His Majesty the Maharajah Gaj
Sing Ji, Henriette Gaillard, Jean and Isabelle Garçon, John MacGlenaghan, Fiora Gondolfi, Annick Goutal
and Alain Meunier, Murielle Grateau, Yves and Michèle Halard, Hotel Le Sénéchal, Hotel Samod Haveli,
Anthony Hudson, Ann Huybens, Patrick T'Hoft, Igor and Lili, Michèle Iodice, Paul Jacquette, Hellson, Jolie
Kelter and Michael Malcé, Dominique Kieffer, Kiwayu, Lawrence and William Kriegel, Philippe Labro, Karl
Lagerfeld, François Lafanour, Nad Laroche, Rudolph Thomas Leimbacher, Philippe Lévèque and Claude
Terrijn, Marion Lesage, Luna, Catherine Margaretis, Marongiu, Mathias, Valérie Mazerat and Bernard
Ghèzy, Jean-Louis Mennesson, Ilaria Miani, Anna Moï, Leonardo Mondadori, Jacqueline Morabito,
Christine Moussière, Paola Navone, Christine Nicaise, Christian Neirynck, Jean Oddes, Catherine Painvin,
John Pawson, Christiane Perrochon, Phong Pfeufer, Françoise Pialoux les Terrasses, Alberto Pinto, Stéphane
Plassier, Morgan Puett, Riad Dar Amane, Riad Dar Kawa, Yagura Rié, Guillaume Saalburg, Holly Salomon,
Jocelyne and Jean-Louis Sibuet, Siegrid and her cousins, Valérie Solvi, Richard Texier, Jérôme Tisné, Doug
Tomkins, Anna and Patrice Touron, Christian Tortu, Armand Ventilo, Barbara de Vries, Thomas Wegner,
Quentin Wilbaux, Catherine Willis.

Thanks are also due to the following magazines for allowing me to include photographs originally published
by them: *Architectural Digest* (French Edition), *Atmosphère, Elle, Elle à Table, Elle Décoration, Elle Décor
Italie, Madame Figaro, Maison Française, Marie Claire, Marie Claire Idées, Marie Claire Maison, The World of
Interiors.*

Gilles de Chabaneix